D1630506

Wheels of Fortune

Self-funding Infrastructure and
the Free Market Case for a Land Tax

Wheels of Fortune

Self-funding Infrastructure and
the Free Market Case for a Land Tax

FRED HARRISON

FOREWORD BY DON RILEY

The Institute of Economic Affairs

First published in Great Britain in 2006 by
The Institute of Economic Affairs
2 Lord North Street
Westminster
London SW1P 3LB
in association with Profile Books Ltd

The mission of the Institute of Economic Affairs is to improve public understanding of the fundamental institutions of a free society, with particular reference to the role of markets in solving economic and social problems.

A CIP catalogue record for this book is available from the British Library.

ISBN 0 255 36589 6

Many IEA publications are translated into languages other than English or are reprinted. Permission to translate or to reprint should be sought from the Director General at the address above.

Typeset in Stone by MacGuru Ltd
info@macguru.org.uk
Printed and bound in Great Britain by Hobbs the Printers

CONTENTS

The author   10
Foreword by Don Riley   11
Introduction   16
Acknowledgements   19
Summary   20
List of tables, figures and boxes   22

1 Of leakages and losses   25
The making of a contradiction   25
Unbalanced books   29
Postponing the future   32
The doctrine of market failure   38

2 The dis-integrated economy   45
The planning and policy nexus   45
Surrogate signals   51
Whose money is it anyway?   56
The rent barometer   60

3 Free trains or free riders?   64
Reichmann's windfall train   64
Turf wars   69
Dividing the spoils   76

The free riders   78

4 Far Eastern promises   83
Infrascapes   83
Hong Kong: a colonial legacy   87
Singapore: bidding for space   94
Japan: shopping for efficiency   97

5 The rent-optimising goal   106
The dynamics of location   106
'A peculiar tax'   111
All roads lead to Rome   115
Markets as society's mediator   118

6 The culture of statism   122
Counter-factual history   122
The Stockton and Darlington Railway   124
The transport confidence trick   128
Rolling back the state   132

7 The politics of economics   135
Highways: waste not, want not   135
Airways: appropriating the skies   139
The corruption of enterprise   144
Pricing amenities in social spaces   151

8 Accounting for democratic governance   155
The First Law of Social Dynamics   155
Paying for benefits received   161

Accounting for leakages and losses   164
Retiring the bad taxes   169

References   176

About the IEA   186

The English are incurious as to theory, take fundamentals for granted and are more interested in the state of the roads than in their place on the map.

R. H. Tawney

Dedicated to the memory of
JOHN HARRISON,
whose journey ended prematurely,
on the road to Mafeking,
9 March 1994

THE AUTHOR

Fred Harrison is a graduate of the universities of Oxford and London. His career in journalism was followed by a period of ten years working in Russia, where he advised the Duma and municipal governments on free market-based fiscal reform. He is author of *The Power in the Land* (1983) and co-author (with Mason Gaffney) of *The Corruption of Economics* (1994). His most recent publication is *Boom Bust: House Prices, Banking and the Depression of 2010* (2005). He is Research Director of the London-based Land Research Trust.

FOREWORD

As the author of *Taken for a Ride* (Riley, 2001), and someone who personally benefited from the huge increases in land values that resulted from the publicly funded construction of the Jubilee Line extension through South London in the late 1990s, I am delighted to have been asked to write this foreword to Fred Harrison's important new monograph, which considers how increases in the value of land resulting from large infrastructure projects may be captured in order to fund such projects.

I landed at Dover after a choppy crossing of the Channel in 1962, and for the next 40 years I paid my taxes to Her Majesty's Treasury. Working in the computer industry, I spent some years in the Soviet Union – but still, when resident in the UK, I did not dodge my obligations to the public purse. After all, I was married, raising two children and using the public services; so I was happy to pay my share of the costs of the schools and hospitals that my family needed.

Then, as the millennium was dawning, a miracle happened. The government returned every penny that I had paid in taxes over the previous 40 years. So for four decades I had lived tax-free – and I had not dodged the taxman! How was this possible? I 'confessed' in *Taken for a Ride*. Taxpayers generously funded the extension to the Jubilee Line, one of London's Underground lines. Two of the stations were located close to office properties that I own. Those two stations raised the value of my properties by more than all the taxes that I had paid into the public's coffers over the previous 40 years.

A nice windfall for this colonial boy.

Did it make sense for Britain's taxpayers?

It did not. And that set me wondering. It was symptomatic of the perverse taxes that governments use to fund the capital infrastructure of systems such as the transport network. What was Rome's secret? How could it build highways on a global scale?

Two thousand years ago, the Romans created a self-funded global network of 10,000 kilometres of roads stretching north–south from Hibernia through Rome to Damascus.

The Romans utilised investment talents stretching back to the first civilisations in the Near East. From then to the 21st century, except for rare periods of enlightenment, an economic darkness descended on Europe.

Now, in 2005, the City of London, with all the prestige, wealth, brainpower and engineering strengths at its disposal, seems unable to rediscover (reinvent) the 4,000-year-old economic investment model, to dig out and equip a modest 15-kilometre east–west tunnel.

In the 1950s, I could have known how it might be done, because I spent many an hour sitting on the evidence while going to university in New Zealand. The locomotives of the Wellington and Manawatu Railway Co. traverse some of the loveliest countryside in the world. It was constructed with private money at a cost of £767,665. The last section – extending the line to Paekakariki – was opened in 1886. It paid annual dividends to its shareholders until the government purchased it in 1908.

That great railway success is an economic lesson for governments today. The railway did more than deliver goods and passengers across the gorges that slice through North Island. In the seventeen years after the first trains steamed out of Wellington, the value of land along its route increased by £4 million, according to the *New Zealand Times*.

One of the men responsible for the railroad, Sir Julius Vogel, proposed that the community should retain alternate sections along the route. This sensible proposal was rejected for reasons that were documented by Michael Flürscheim, a German industrialist of the nineteenth century. He (like the chocolate kings George Cadbury and Joseph Rowntree in Britain) turned philanthropist, and he helped his employees to enjoy a good standard of living before packing his bags and migrating to New Zealand. There, he campaigned for reform of the way in which infrastructure was funded. He had learnt that the enterprise economy would be best served if locational values were tapped to fund the investments.

In the case of the Wellington and Manawatu Railway, if the Vogel plan had been adopted, the land would have been rented out to the settlers from Europe who landed on the quaysides of Wellington. Two consequences would have followed, both of potentially historic significance.

First, there would have been no need for the colonial government to tax private enterprise. Second, the railway could have been funded out of four years' rental income from the land whose value it raised. This would have been a painless way to fund the infrastructure that was needed to tap the resources of these virgin territories – or, as Fred Harrison puts it, the *self-funding* solution to the provision of the shared services that communities need. Flürscheim illustrated the mechanism of this self-funding strategy: it was based on the principle on which elevators are operated by the owners of skyscrapers – 'whose free use is given to the public, the increased rent of the offices more than paying for the expense'.[1]

Flürscheim (n.d.: 94) explained why this did not happen:

> Private speculators were too powerful to allow such a scheme to pass, and private speculators have pocketed the millions of increment created through the new roads. It is not too much to say that if the community had kept the land alongside the roads, only leasing it at periodical revaluations, instead of selling the fee simple, by this time the entire debt contracted for the roads would be paid off.

History offers important lessons for governments that need more efficient strategies than the failed formulas of the twentieth century. It appears that any solution must embrace this principle: the 'free riders' need to be turned into paying passengers. How this might be achieved is the subject of this book.

Fred Harrison has not invented a new approach to funding infrastructure. But modern governments have forgotten the formula that was worked out by the peoples of antiquity.

- The peasant cultivators of the first civilisations, those in the Near East, pooled resources through their temples to create canals. These irrigated their fields and were the highways down which their produce was transported to markets.
- The Romans used a similar principle, but they worked through the secular city institutions to build their roads. These arteries, on dry land, were the lifeblood of the greatest empire on earth.

---

1   The economics of the elevator are discussed in Foldvary (2005: 25).

Modern Europeans – notably the Portuguese, Spanish, British and Dutch – built their civilisation through communication networks on the high seas. The riches of other continents were extracted and loaded on to the sailing ships that braved the storms to land their cargoes on the quaysides of Portsmouth and Antwerp. The main cost was the harbours and the naval vessels to protect the shipping lanes.

As routes of communication, the oceans cost little or nothing to provide access to the spices and precious metals – and, yes, the slaves – of other lands. The energy required by the sailing ships – the winds and currents – were nature's free gift. Some of the leading aristocratic families of Europe were fabulously enriched.

Then something astonishing happened. The British aristocracy discovered that it could get rich without incurring the risks of ocean storms and plundering pirates. Relocating the wealth-creating activity on their home territories could deliver huge windfall gains – without having to work for them. The treasures were beneath their feet, and the riches expanded as capital was invested in transport within the United Kingdom. But someone had to pay for the infrastructure that made possible the new systems of transportation. That is the story which unfolds in this monograph.

DON RILEY

INTRODUCTION

It is often assumed that government intervention is required to bring to fruition large-scale infrastructure projects, such as the construction of railway lines or sewerage systems. In particular, government involvement is believed to be necessary to provide the large initial capital outlays such projects require.

In *Wheels of Fortune*, Fred Harrison shows that large-scale infrastructure projects can be made self-funding and hence be completed without recourse to public funds.

Infrastructure projects almost always bring about a large increase in the value of adjoining land. For example, Transport for London estimate that the extension of the Jubilee Line of the London Underground that opened in 1999 increased land values by £2 billion in Canary Wharf and £800 million in Southwark. When such infrastructure projects are funded by government they therefore almost always involve a substantial transfer of wealth from a large number of taxpayers to a small number of property owners.

Demands that government should fund infrastructure projects often come from those who would benefit – either directly from, for example, cheaper public transport or indirectly from increased property values. Such demands may be characterised as rent-seeking – an attempt to use the political process to achieve an economic gain.

Hence, when MPs representing the outer London suburbs call for public funding of a project like Crossrail that would benefit their constituents by providing quicker journey times into the capital and increasing the value of their properties, such politicians are engaging in rent-seeking on behalf of their constituents by attempting to force taxpayers throughout the country to pay for a project that will disproportionately benefit their (often already wealthy) constituents.

Harrison argues that a fairer and more efficient means to fund infrastructure projects is to capture and use the increases in land values that they bring. Indeed, Harrison describes how the initial proposal for the Jubilee Line extension made by property owners at Canary Wharf involved funding the project with private finance put up against anticipated rises in property values. Had this option been pursued the entire project could have been completed at no cost to the public purse.

In this monograph, Harrison sets out a free market case for a form of land tax as a means of achieving the goal of self-funding infrastructure and ensuring that those who receive the benefits of such projects meet the costs. He shows the antecedents of the land tax idea in the work of the classical economists, notably Smith and Ricardo, and demonstrates how other countries, in particular Singapore and Hong Kong, have better utilised the value of land as the foundation for their economic prosperity.

Harrison does not shy away from the more challenging practicalities of a land tax. In particular, he addresses the problem of ascertaining the contribution of different phenomena to a property's value. Given that the value of any good, service or factor is not objectively given but is always a subjective judgement based on each individual's personal preferences, this must be the most important practical challenge to a workable land tax.

From a free market perspective it is also important that a land tax should not become yet another tax added to the already burgeoning tax burden. The introduction of a land tax must coincide with the repeal of a number of existing taxes – Harrison proposes that it replaces economically damaging capital gains and income taxes. It also has to be noted that any reassignment of the tax burden is likely to be highly politically controversial; those countries where land tax regimes work successfully have a long history of this form of taxation.

The key to the future of self-funding infrastructure, then, may be to construct (or allow to evolve) a regime of private property rights that allows the benefits of such projects to be captured and thereby prevents rent-seeking by relatively small groups of property owners at the expense of other taxpayers. There is strong empirical evidence presented in this monograph to suggest that a land tax could provide a way forward to such a future.

If this were to happen, the resulting change would not necessarily be akin to a tax, but more like the service charge for shared amenities that the owners of a shopping mall may charge those leasing individual units.

As in all IEA publications, the views expressed in Hobart Paper 154 are those of the author, not those of the Institute (which has no corporate view), its managing trustees, Academic Advisory Council or senior staff.

JOHN MEADOWCROFT
Deputy Editorial Director,
Institute of Economic Affairs
January 2006

ACKNOWLEDGEMENTS

The wise counsel offered by Dr Rana Roy and Professor Nicolaus Tideman is acknowledged with gratitude. Many people were generous with their assistance, but special thanks are due to Dave Wetzel, Vicky Jennings, James Muldowney and Michael Schabas. A research grant from the Robert Schalkenbach Foundation of New York enabled the author to explore the formative role of transport infrastructure in the expansion of the US West. The usual disclaimer applies: the author bears all responsibility for errors and omissions.

The IEA would like to acknowledge the generous support of Don Riley for this publication.

SUMMARY

- The prevalence of the myth that large-scale infrastructure projects can be brought to fruition only through government intervention to fund the initial capital outlay such projects require has led to chronic under-investment in the UK's transport infrastructure.

- Where infrastructure projects have been attempted without public money in the UK, such as in the construction of the Channel Tunnel, post-completion operating revenues have often been insufficient to repay the debt accrued by the initial capital expenditure. Such problems result principally from the economic model utilised in such projects rather than an inherent inability of such projects to be self-funding.

- Infrastructure projects almost always bring about an increase in the value of adjoining land. For example, it is estimated that the London Underground Jubilee Line extension increased land values by close to £3 billion around just two stations. When such projects are publicly funded, this represents a substantial transfer of wealth from taxpayers to local property owners. Hence, government funding of infrastructure projects may be a form of rent-seeking in which already wealthy property owners have the value of their properties multiplied via the public purse.

- The present method of funding infrastructure projects in the

UK is inefficient, leading to the under-supply of such projects, and is unfair, leading to the unequal distribution of the costs and benefits that accrue.

- The experience of other countries shows that more efficient and fairer regimes for funding infrastructure projects can be developed. Hong Kong, Japan and Singapore have utilised the value of land to fund the construction and maintenance of extremely efficient, modern transport systems that now operate successfully without taxpayers' money: modern, efficient transport systems do not necessarily require public subsidy.

- A similar approach should be adopted in the UK, in which some of the increases in land values that result from infrastructure projects are captured and used to fund such projects.

- At present it is estimated that for every £1 of tax raised by the government, as much as £2 of wealth is lost to the economy as a result of the opportunity cost of activities forgone. A more efficient and fairer tax system would reduce this net loss of wealth and the welfare it would bring.

- The introduction of a land tax and/or user charging for transport services combined with the retirement of a number of existing taxes would minimise the loss to the economy resulting from inefficient and harmful forms of taxation.

- Reassigning the tax burden from capital and labour to land would enable many existing taxes to be abolished, would reduce the deadweight losses resulting from taxation and would enable market mechanisms to more accurately reflect the costs and benefits of the provision of different goods and services. In short, it would lead to the development of a fairer and more efficient model of capitalism.

TABLES, FIGURES AND BOXES

Table 1	Value-for-money criteria	30
Table 2	Diminishing expectations: UK trunk road plans	40
Table 3	Vital statistics of selected countries	85
Table 4	Road realities (1998)	95
Table 5	The 10-Year Transport Plan	168
Table 6	Revenue and welfare changes from optimal pricing	171
Table 7	Cost recovery from optimal pricing	172
Figure 1	The social model of production	109
Box 1	The Crossrail conundrum	36
Box 2	The capital costs of transport	37
Box 3	Rent and the consumer's surplus	54
Box 4	The philosophy of property	90
Box 5	The sin of omission	114
Box 6	Efficiency gains from rental payments	137
Box 7	The historic reality	166

Wheels of Fortune

Self-funding Infrastructure and
the Free Market Case for a Land Tax

1   OF LEAKAGES AND LOSSES

The making of a contradiction

Karl Marx was correct on one point. There is a contradiction at the heart of capitalism. His error was in ascribing responsibility to private markets. Our competing hypothesis locates systemic failure in public policy.

If state investment, welfare and regulation are supposed to compensate for shortcomings in the market economy, their notable failures suggest the need for a fresh appraisal. Why, for example, has the gap between the rich and the poor, which was supposed to be narrowed by progressive taxes, not narrowed? The gap remains as large today as when the Beveridge Plan was institutionalised as the welfare state 60 years ago (Womack, 2005, quoting the results of Roberts, 2005). What has gone wrong is not *explained* by conventional analytical models, because these ignore the principles that underpin the optimisation of the wealth and the welfare of the nation. Where are the points of friction that impede the efficient allocation of resources and income?

To concentrate our investigation, we shall focus on the funding and operation of mass transit systems. We shall drill a test bore hole into the economy to scrutinise the vital core of capitalism. The efficiency of mass production was contingent on the way products were distributed when they came off the conveyor belts.

By examining the way transport is funded, we magnify the structural weaknesses that compromise the operations of markets.

Despite two hundred years of advances in technology and finance, there is a serious deficiency in the supply and quality of infrastructure. Britain alone needs a huge increase in investment in infrastructure if the private sector is to meet the challenges of the globalised economy. There would be no shortage of funding if government adopted efficient methods of raising the public's revenue. The studies we discuss in Chapter 8 reveal that the *increase* in revenues would have been about £24 billion per annum – *after* retiring £37 billion of conventional taxes that are currently imposed on transport (Roy, 2005). This is part of the dividend from tax reform, the additional flow of riches that is within the nation's grasp if the British government chooses to be as financially efficient at its business (the stewardship of the public purse) as it expects the private sector to be in discharging its responsibilities. Britain lacks enough money to invest in the infrastructure the nation needs because of bad governance.

Transport is associated with problems in both the public and the private sectors. This suggests interdependence between the two sectors that cannot be resolved by a theory focused exclusively on private markets or on public goods. A more complex approach is required that integrates the two into a comprehensive model. Equipped with a richer theory, we hope to resolve some currently intractable difficulties. For example, mass transportation originated with the genius of individuals and the investment of private capital. Why, then, is there a consensus today that highways and railways cannot be profitable for private investors? This contention legitimises subsidies from the taxpayer to support private enterprise.

Our historical analysis (Chapters 4 and 6) will show that transport systems *can* and *do* pay for themselves without the need for subsidies from taxpayers. This conclusion is based on a full audit of the performance of the value-adding economy. The evidence is examined in terms of policies elucidated by Adam Smith in the eighteenth century, and in particular the neglected aspects of his insights into optimum policies for funding governance and the enterprise economy.

The formative period for free enterprise was the nineteenth century. Industry operated with the minimum of intervention by the state. If the economy did not work efficiently in a legal and institutional environment that was virtually free of state regulation, macroeconomic instability cannot be attributed to direct government involvement in the way markets operate. We know that the railway industry, for example, was severely disrupted in the middle of the nineteenth century as a result of large-scale bankruptcies among banks and investors. Was this the result of a defect in the value-adding market economy, or was the state responsible by default? Did it fail to discharge its obligations to all citizens, and as a consequence favour a select minority?

To test the efficacy of public policy, we move on to the twentieth century. The unprecedented engagement of government in economic affairs in the last 60 years has failed to resolve problems that surfaced in the nineteenth century. This suggests that public policy may have been fatally flawed; if so, the flashpoints ought to attract our attention.

• In the nineteenth century, there was enormous leakage of value out of the value-adding layer of the economy. If the majority did not benefit, who did gain from the technological advances in mass transport systems?

Private enterprise was viable if it could cover its costs of production from the prices that could be charged to customers. But there was one exception to the rule that people would be rewarded out of the value they added to total incomes. Parliament sanctioned the leakage as a charge for the use of land or natural resources. The law facilitated this charge (rent) as a *transfer payment*. By this term, I mean a transaction in which the rent receiver's gain was the rent payer's loss. It was not a payment for a reciprocal product or service delivered by the landowner, per se, but a mere transfer of income from one party to another.[1]

If rent payments were a haemorrhage of value – a continuous leak, hour after hour – out of the possession of the investors and employees who created it, we would expect systemic crises of the kind that would one day create the demand for compensatory action by the state. This leads us to the second flashpoint.

- In the twentieth century, the state's attempts to correct social and economic problems were based on the redistribution of income through taxation. But this remedial action caused serious state-sponsored losses.

Compensatory action by the tax state – the attempt to ameliorate the human tragedies that were documented during the Victorian era – came at a price. The technical term for this price is the Social

---

1   Rent, because of its complexity, does not conform to the strict economic definition of a transfer, which is a payment for which nothing is provided in return. Our use differs from transfers in both the private sector (in which a gift is a voluntary bequest) and the public sector (such as transfers to people in need, including the disabled or unemployed). With rent, the payer receives a benefit (the services associated with the land); but the recipient of rent is not the provider of the services whose value is reflected in the value of land.

Opportunity Cost of Exchequer Funds (SOCEF). Governments raised revenue by using tools that damaged the economy, communities and the natural environment. The expenditure of money through the public sector yielded lower returns than if the money had been invested by people in the markets. What prevented policy-makers from adopting policies that avoided such damage? Did such policies exist?

In our view, these two vitriolic flashpoints – the *leakages* from the private sector and the *losses* caused by the public sector – combined to impose artificial ceilings on the productive potential of the nation.

Unbalanced books

Despite a century of democratic politics, government has not overcome the problems that are associated with the services that are essential for a highly mobile population that works in a dynamic economy. These problems are linked to the need to lock up capital in canals, roads and railways for long periods of time. Much of that capital cost is now shifted on to taxpayers. But government has not proved to be more reliable than nineteenth-century private enterprises in handling the funding of infrastructure. Furthermore, government itself is now a restraint on investment.

Orwellian language is used to disguise the sources of the problem. One example relates to the way assessments are made on whether to invest taxpayers' money. Policy-makers acclaim themselves for delivering 'value for money'. For Britain, the terms of this principle were specified by the Department for Transport in 2004. Projects with a benefit-to-cost ratio of more than 2:1 might

Table 1 **Value-for-money criteria**

Value-for-money category	Benefit-to-cost ratio	Prospects for projects
Poor	Less than 1	None
Low	Between 1 and 1.5	Very few
Medium	Between 1.5 and 2	Some, but by no means all
High	Over 2	Most, if not all

Source: Department for Transport, 2004: paras 15 and 31

fall by the wayside. A facility that could yield up to £2 in benefits for £1 invested by the taxpayer is rejected (see Table 1)! Private investors would flock to fund projects that would double their money. Why should government disallow projects that would yield a similar return?

When taxpayers' money is spent, allowance has to be made for 'the distortionary impacts of general taxation on the economy' (Department for Transport, 2004: para. 13). The yardstick employed by HM Treasury for the damage it causes is 30p in every £1 raised through taxes. So a benefit-to-cost ratio of 1.05:1, that is a 5 per cent return on capital, which would be acceptable to private investors, is a dead loss when taxpayers' money is invested. The minimum 'break even' return has to be 1.3:1 (a return of 30 per cent) for a tax-funded project. But this apparent balancing of a public venture's books would not eliminate the damage to the private sector as a result of the way government raised its revenue.[2] *Distortionary taxes create an artificial barrier between people and the amenities they need.* Services for which people would be willing to pay if they were delivered by private enterprise are unviable when funded by government. This explains why some projects that would yield a handsome profit to the private sector (a 30 per cent

2   In fact, the damage is appreciably higher than the 30p-in-the-pound yardstick employed by the British government. See Chapter 8.

return would be welcomed as a magnificent return on capital) are disqualified when funded by taxpayers' money, leaving the public bereft of services it needs.

Government, of course, is not anxious to publicise its role as a predator. Language is manipulated to camouflage the politically sanctioned obstacles that are placed in the way of the provision of public goods. Thus, we are told that investment in transport is curbed because we live 'in a world of constrained resources' (ibid.: para. 31). Why, when we could make goods and deliver services to the point of satiation, is there a shortage when we need them? Is this claim tenable for governments that claim to operate on the basis of value for people's money? If an investment in transport can cover all its costs, why should it be denied to those who are willing to pay for it? Could this state-sponsored constraint on investment be the cause of the sclerosis that was evident in the twentieth-century economy?

But private markets did break down on a cyclical basis (Harrison, 2005). This suggests that there is something amiss with the economics of the private sector. But does this instability ultimately originate from the same source as inefficiency in the public sector? Would a single remedy resolve problems in both sectors? We shall approach this issue by asking: if the public and private sectors were meant to work in partnership in the transport sector, why is this partnership unable to deliver affordable quality services to the people who need them? Is there something defective in the financial architecture that binds the two sectors together? We shall show that the distortions of taxation are the common source of the problem. Adam Smith proposed a policy that avoided such distortions (see Chapter 5).

Postponing the future

The fate of Britain's transport networks is a cause for concern among some who work in the industry. One such person is Richard Bowker. He was chairman of the government's Strategic Rail Authority (SRA) until September 2004. He was awarded a CBE for the services he rendered to the rail industry.

In Bowker's view, the hurdles created by value-for-money assessments mean that people outside the M25 ring road which circles London can forget any meaningful investment in their regions. But could the problem be less to do with the availability of money and more to do with his claim that 'much of the theory is accepted fact'? (Bowker, 2005: 34). For example, is it empirically correct that 'Railways, as a rule, don't make money overall'? There is good historical evidence with which to challenge this assertion. From the first railway in Darlington in the 1830s to the regional railways of the 1960s, the movement of people and goods yielded returns that more than paid for operating costs and the infra-structure (see Chapters 2, 4, 6 and 8). This evidence was apparently unknown to the head of the SRA, who boldly claimed: 'In the mid-1960s, it was obvious to just about everyone that the days of railway companies making enough profit from operations to cover their cost of capital, and still return a dividend to shareholders, were gone' (ibid.: 35).

Paradoxically, this assessment would probably have been regarded as correct by shareholders at the end of the Victorian era. How can we explain this disconnection between the finan-cial facts and the golden age of rail? Was the apparent shortfall in revenue and perpetual crisis of scores of UK and US independent rail companies due to the incompetence of entrepreneurs? Why were they not able to create sufficient value to cover the cost of capital and pay dividends? We shall show that their financial problems were the result of leakages of value out of the hands of the inventors and shareholders who created it.

Having lost the battle to balance the books, railway operators have now resigned themselves to the role of supplicants. They turn to government for tax-funded subsidies to cover the cost of rail infrastructure. The language they use disguises the underlying economic realities, and camouflages viable alternative ways of funding the rail industry.

The Industrial Revolution delivered a new order of scale in both commerce and finance. There was a giant leap in the manufacture of products for sale to a global market of consumers. But the promise of prosperity for all was contingent on a new kind of physical infrastructure. For progress in productivity to be fully realised it was necessary for the governing class to re-evaluate property rights and public finance. Their empirical guide ought to have been the experiences that emerged in the revolution in mobility that was made possible by the canals of the eighteenth century.

Problems did not originate with the need to cover operating costs in the railway industry. Fare and freight charges, adjusted through competition, were sufficient to defray the costs of rolling stock and the wages of men to man the engines and to shovel the coal that fuelled the fires that generated the steam. *The problem was with the capital that had to be locked up in the infrastructure – the land, tracks and station buildings.* The failure to understand the economics of infrastructure exacted a terrible price on those who entrusted their money to capital-hungry enterprises. A classic contemporary example is the Channel Tunnel.

For nearly one thousand years the British Isles have been

safeguarded by the English Channel. The crossing by boat had been made, notably by the Romans in biblical times and the Normans a millennium later. But the White Cliffs of Dover were an effective rampart against other marauders. When Margaret Thatcher decided to breach those defences with a tunnel beneath the sea, she ruled that taxpayers should not foot the bill.

In 2004, Eurotunnel's chief executive, Richard Shirrefs, blamed Thatcher for the financial crisis that befell the Anglo-French company that owned the tunnel. It could not meet the interest payments on its £6-billion-plus debt. The reason, explained Shirrefs, was that 'She put a private company into existence which almost from day one was destined to have a financial problem. The industry model is in a state of failure. It just doesn't work, obviously' (Clark, 2004).

Investors ranged from financial institutions to a million French citizens who ended up as owners of shares in the corporation that charged rent for railway operators such as Eurostar to run their trains on its tracks.

The tunnel linking England and France was one of the major engineering feats of the twentieth century. But investors lost their savings as the value of their shares plummeted lower than the two holes through which trains now whistle back and forth. The financial disaster was inevitable because the financial architecture was inferior to the technical skills of the excavators who burrowed beneath the seabed.

Eurotunnel makes an operating profit.[3] Its customers appreciate the service they receive and they are willing to pay what it costs to transport people and freight between Britain and the

---

3   Eurotunnel's operating profit rose to £171 million in 2004. This was wiped out by net interest charges of £298 million.

Continent. But market prices could not deliver sufficient revenue to repay Eurotunnel's capital debt. The reason they could not do so is testimony to the *success* of market processes. Competition from sea-borne traffic and low-cost airlines prevents Eurotunnel from exacting a monopoly price for its service. If it had been in a privileged position to do so, it could have covered the cost of capital. But even so, does the tunnel create sufficient additional value – the rents that are not captured by Eurotunnel's prices – that at least equates with the costs of capital?[4]

Why were the French and British governments emphatic that the tunnel had to be funded by the private sector? One reason flowed from another piece of conventional wisdom. Bowker (2005: 36) expressed this in terms of the need to ration the use of taxpayers' money. The pressure on government to control its borrowing arose because 'there simply isn't the money, so the capital is rationed. Techniques exist to ration this capital on an economically rational and equitable basis'.

The techniques for rationing capital, while they may be arithmetically rational, are certainly not administered in an equitable way. If we are correct – if amenities like railway systems are self-funding – there is little sense in the claim that the money does not exist to provide the infrastructure we need (see Box 1).

It is true that governments cannot satisfy all the demands that are made upon them. Special interest groups constantly increase the burdens on the state budget. The outcome is financial stress.

4   Rent is generated by (i) nature (for which there is no social cost: as with fish in the sea, coal beneath the ground, which are 'freely provided by nature'); (ii) the community (as in the locational decisions that people collectively make on where to live and what to invest in their communities); and (iii) private activity (as with the individual who devised the Internet, which gave added rental value to the radio spectrum).

Box 1 **The Crossrail conundrum**

The confusion in the language and theory of public investment is illustrated by London's Crossrail project. The benefits eclipse the costs of this proposed railway linking west with east London by a ratio of 2:1. 'Fabulous!' exclaimed Richard Bowker. 'So why haven't we done it? Because ten billion pounds, after adjusting for risk, is a heck of lot [*sic*] of money and big decisions take longer. Apparently.'

With funding spread over the years of construction, £10 billion is a trivial sum in relation to the benefits that would accrue to the London economy. And as for the delay in making a decision, London's need for Crossrail was identified as early as the 1940s! The failure to build it has nothing to do with the speed with which politicians can make decisions. The problem is with the methodology employed by transport planners. But this methodology is biased to accommodate flaws in some of the buttresses that support capitalism.

Governments that cannot fund current spending commitments out of tax revenue resort to borrowing. This compromises the operational efficiency of the economy. Borrowing to spend on ballooning welfare demands crowds out borrowing for investment in infrastructure. Indebted governments cannot default on their debts, but they can erode the value of the currency by printing more notes.

Today, to postpone inflation and secure the appearance of prudence, the Treasury encourages the funding of public projects out of private finance. In many cases, it now transpires, these are

Box 2 **The capital costs of transport**

The Corporation of London's Economic Development Office reported that 'transport has emerged as the No 1 concern of City businesses, irrespective of the topic actually being researched'.* Oxford Economic Forecasting (OEF) estimated the effects of the dilapidated transport systems that existed in the capital in 2002. Depending on the values placed on a person's time, OEF conservatively calculated that delays in travel cost £230 million every year. Adding the cost of the leisure time of city workers raised the loss to £575 million.

In 2003, when Mayor Ken Livingstone was granted control of the capital's Tube, his Transport for London defined no fewer than 20 major transport schemes. When in place, the new bridges, roads, trams and trains would equip the capital to take on all comers. But according to Transport Commissioner Bob Kiley: 'There is not one project that people have heard about in this town that will happen right now, because they are not funded. Not one of them.' He warned that years of neglect of the capital's infrastructure required a catch-up strategy costing an additional £900 million every year.

But instead of raising investment, the government proposed to spend less than was required. Kiley noted: 'Bizarrely, its grants are to be reduced by £1 billion over the 2004–10 period. The result will be more congested roads, greater overcrowding on the Tube, a decline in bus use and an overall fall in service reliability.'[†]

---

* *City Research Focus*, Corporation of London, London, October 2003, p. 5.
† Bob Kiley, 'London's route to better transport', *Financial Times*, 3 December 2003.

not legitimate 'off balance sheet' projects for the public sector.[5] The arbitrary manipulation of statistics in the national accounts, however, does nothing to overcome the shortfall in the funding of infrastructure. In the transport sector, policy continues to short-change travellers and the businesses that require efficient modes of communication (see Box 2).

The doctrine of market failure

Transmission mechanisms that link private enterprise with infrastructure need to be synchronised. The financial causeways suffer from sclerotic blockages that impede the flow of the information that is required to ensure optimum efficiency. One victim is the pricing mechanism, which is the market's information highway. It is a conduit that cannot operate effectively while taxes are loaded on to product prices.

Governments advocate the need for sustainable solutions, but no fundamental changes have been introduced to justify the claim that they are more efficient than the private sector at delivering the projects that people need. This is not for want of knowledge that comes from large-scale social experiments such as changes to the ownership of Britain's rail network.

From their origins as private enterprises in the nineteenth century, railways capitulated and were nationalised as British Rail in 1948. They were then reprivatised in 1993 under the umbrella

---

5   The Office for National Statistics (ONS) initiated research to identify capital expenditure undertaken under the Private Finance Initiative (PFI) which ought to be included in public sector net debt figures. By the end of 2004, PFI projects were valued at £42.7 billion. The ONS was reported to be considering the reclassification of 57 per cent of these projects as 'on balance sheet' because little risk had been transferred to the private sector (Giles, 2005).

of Railtrack, which owned the infrastructure. The great restoration failed. The financial model on which they operated had not matured sufficiently to detach them from the milk that flowed from the bosom of the taxpayer. Railtrack was forced out of the private sector and into the hybrid not-for-profit Network Rail. This continues to receive tax-funded subsidies to cover capital costs.[6] Far from this being the end of the line, we suspect that the rail industry has been parked in a convenient siding while planners consult their crystal balls.[7]

Progress is, however, unlikely until we understand the dynamics of the implosive process that is built into the economy. As population increases and expectations rise, governments are even less able to cope with the demands upon them. The result is a continuous deterioration in their ability to maintain the required levels of investment, a situation that is periodically 'corrected' in response to explosions of social discontent. There are two aspects to this process, that of *under*-investment in the right places and *over*-investment in the wrong places. Both stem directly from the leakages-and-losses nexus.

The future is being compromised by under-investment. A continuous process of contraction is at work in which the social space we inhabit is systematically impoverished. One measure of this under-investment has been offered for Britain by Rana

6   Network Rail reported an improvement in its financial performance in 2004/05, as well it might with the benefit of what the *Guardian* (27 May 2005) called 'the whirligig of subsidies'. About 54 per cent of Network Rail's turnover of £3.8 billion came from direct government grants and revenue from the franchise rail operators of £1.4 billion, part of which was subsidies from the public purse.

7   In June 2005, Network Rail was criticised by the chairman of the Office of Rail Regulation for under-spending nearly £1 billion; the money had been allocated to upgrade the rail network. Chris Bolt wanted 'to make sure ... that Network Rail is not storing up problems for the future' (Clark, 2005).

Table 2 **Diminishing expectations: UK trunk road plans**

	Number of proposed schemes	Cost (£ billion)
1989	500	17
1994	400	24
1995	300	16
1997	147	6
2000	21	?

Sources: House of Commons Transport Select Committee (2003: 5); Department of the Environment, Transport and the Regions (2000)

Roy. Examining the record of the last 20 years, he found that the downward trends in public investment had not been reversed by the Blair government since 1997; on the contrary, he highlights 'a near-continuous decline in net public investment' (Roy, 2003: 6). The annual shortfall in the years under New Labour was something like £7 billion compared with the previous decade. Transport policy reflects the financial logic of the system. There remains a clear gap between declared intentions and the plans to deliver investment in infrastructure.[8] This is suggested by the diminishing expectations in the sphere of trunk roads (Table 2).

Motorists are bewildered by the indecisiveness over plans for highways. Environmentalists might favour the explanation that the decline in the number of proposed schemes is driven by a heightened sensitivity to the nation's ecology, and the determination to shift people and goods on to railways. That thesis is not plausible when viewed in terms of the chaos in the planning system (see Chapter 2). The diminishing expectations can be explained by the propensity to under-invest as a result of

---

8   The decadal trends in capital formation in the construction sector, which appear to be tied to the fortunes of the business cycle, are reviewed in Harrison (2005: 133).

the dynamics of the leakages and losses that flow from the tax system.

Complementing the under-investment is the over-investment in the wrong locations. The starting point is the government's tax bias against investments that people most need. Projects that are designated as of low and medium value are unlikely to receive funding (see Table 1). That decision *appears* to be in the taxpayer's best interests: money is directed at projects that yield the highest benefits. In fact, the reverse is just as likely to be the case.

Projects that just cover their costs may serve to raise the average rate of return across the economy. This happens when a project supports existing infrastructure, enhancing the use of capital that is already invested. A local economy may not generate super-profits, but it *may* fulfil people's needs, and might do so even more successfully with added layers of investment. But improvements to infrastructure may not be bolted on because the ratio of benefits to costs is insufficient to leapfrog the obstacle created by the government's 30 per cent tax hurdle.

The tax bias favours mega-projects that yield super-profits. A return of 2:1 flows from gigantic investments on low-cost sites that tend to be at a distance from where people live and work. This is why house builders, for example, prefer to develop greenfield sites outside towns, where the rate of return is far higher (because costs are lower) than for construction on reclaimed sites. Across the nation's existing stock of capital, however, average rates of return may be reduced because of under-used investments. *The losses arising from the under-use of resources are not reflected in cost–benefit analyses.*

A prime example is the government's propensity to support urban sprawl with infrastructure that dilutes the efficiency of capital across the nation. Sprawl is driven by the speculative pursuit of windfall profits – that part of transfer payments which is capitalised into the selling price of land.[9] The supply of capital, if it *does* fall short of demand, is made even scarcer by being sunk into under-used transport systems in thinly populated or inappropriately located communities (such as 'dormitory towns'). The investment ought to be concentrated in locations where it would yield the maximum private and social returns while conserving the ecology of economically marginal territories.

The cultural consequences of this process are explored elsewhere (Harrison, 2005). Here we note the economic impact on communities on the spatial margins of society. Instead of increasing the value of existing infrastructure in the relatively lower-productivity regions (where the benefit–cost ratio may be little more than 1:1), the tax bias encourages government to favour high-profile projects serving the centres like London, where the ratio is likely to be 2:1. This under-investment damages the quality of life in peripheral locations like the north-east of England, or Scotland, inducing out-migration that impoverishes the communities that suffer the exodus and overloading the centres that attract people they cannot affordably accommodate. In other words, fiscal policy encourages leapfrogging investment instead of renewing existing communities. The pursuit of capital gains from land (the result of the 'free rider' problem; see Chapter 3) is encouraged by the under-collection of rent from land and the

---

9   Indeed, government itself is responsible for such sprawl. A case in point is the proposed Thames Gateway development of tens of thousands of houses east of London, allegedly to provide affordable homes for 'key workers' who have been priced out of the London housing market. To make green fields and marsh lands habitable, a vast amount of taxpayer-funded infrastructure will be invested in outlying areas in which the social returns are below what they would be if the capital was invested in places where people wanted to live.

over-taxation of wages and interest generated by people and their savings. This discourages investment in capital formation in value-adding enterprises by channelling savings and bank credit into property and financial speculation.

Solutions exist. We can reasonably expect a reform agenda to emerge once people understand that it is possible (*inter alia*) to make trains, planes and automobiles operate on the basis of paying their way in the world. But the willingness to entertain changes will probably not arise until government, Parliament and the community of experts who advise policy-makers can come to terms with the conceptual and methodological flaws in the tools they use to guide the economy.

Remedial action is urgently needed. The evidence that we present is tantamount to an indictment of government. State-sponsored damage by taxation is far worse than the Treasury acknowledges. The 30p/£ ratio (30 per cent) is at the very low end. Economists have offered estimates ranging from 50 per cent to 150 per cent.[10] If we split the difference as a rule-of-thumb guide (100 per cent), government-funded investments need to generate benefits of *more than* 2:1 if the damage caused by taxation is to be offset. This places an almost impossible hurdle in the way of investments that the economy needs when funded through the public sector. And yet, *HM Treasury fails to measure the impact of its policies on the economy*. In answer to an enquiry about the 'excess burden'[11] of its taxes, the Treasury replied: 'The Treasury does not hold any unpublished studies, working papers or any other

10 I owe this to a personal communication from Nicolaus Tideman, professor of economics at Virginia Polytechnic Institute and State University, Blacksburg, Virginia. His work on deadweight losses is reviewed in Chapter 8.

11 This is the technical economic term that economists use to measure the disincentives stemming from taxes which affect people's behaviour.

documentation on the way excess burden estimates are calculated, as you have suggested. Particularly, it would not be the Treasury's role to calculate these.'[12]

Estimates of deadweight losses, notes the Treasury, 'are not very reliable'. And yet, the Treasury declines to improve the estimates so that it can select policies that deliver value for money to the people who pay taxes. Is the Treasury under such an obligation? One would have thought so, for (the present author was informed by the Treasury):

> Although raising revenue is the primary aim of taxation, the Government also has a duty to consider that the taxation system is not wholly neutral, for example, in the context of addressing market failures. How and what is taxed sends clear signals about the economic activities which governments believe should be encouraged and discouraged, and the values they wish to entrench in society.[13]

Thus, while government re-engineers people's lives, it confesses to using taxes whose impact on those lives it does not fully understand, and for which it declines to accept responsibility. The democratic principle of accountability requires a finance ministry to measure the way its actions affect people's lives. This would reveal means of funding investments which do not create distortions in the first place.

The negative impact of taxation is not only at the heart of the crises in transport but within society and the economy as a whole. To prescribe new strategies for the future, using transport as our case study, we must revisit the canal and rail failures of the past.

---

12   E-mail to Fred Harrison from John Adams, Correspondence Manager, HM Treasury, 13 June 2005.
13   Ibid.

2 THE DIS-INTEGRATED ECONOMY

The planning and policy nexus

Planning was supposed to bring order to the economy, efficiency in the use of resources and equity for those who had been
excluded from the riches of the nation. What happened? In terms
of Britain's transport sector, we may turn for some answers to a
committee of parliamentarians.

The Future of the Railway (House of Commons Transport
Select Committee, 2004) was dated 1 April. Its contents were
unbelievable. Was this the ultimate April Fool's Day stunt? The
report by the members of parliament was an excoriating censure
of public agencies. Were these really so incompetent? If not, how
do we explain the comedy of errors documented for the House
of Commons? Taxpayers were being increasingly committed
to subsidising what was supposed to be a private railway, and
decision-making agencies such as the Strategic Rail Authority
(SRA) were tying themselves up in knots through confusion over
lines of authority.

Seasoned politicians, entrepreneurs and railway professionals
administered the network over the ten years following privatisation. They are not fools. And yet, the all-party committee of MPs
exposed the hapless activities of an industry that had seen the
privatised Railtrack go into administration when government

pulled the plug on further subsidies. This was ammunition for those who opposed the sale of state assets. Why did the railway collapse into shameful chaos?

To comprehend what drove the twists and turns of policy, our starting point is the Blair government's £32 million multi-modal studies. The 22 studies were intended to guide integration in the use of cars, buses and railways. In July 2000, the government published *Transport 2010: The 10-Year Plan*, which was promoted with vigour by Deputy Prime Minister John Prescott. The Commons Transport Select Committee investigated the studies and the way in which the decision-makers planned to use the products of the lucrative consultancy projects. Their catalogue of criticisms and revelations does not inspire confidence in the tools of transport planners.

Congestion

Research was concentrated in areas that were deemed to be congested. Alistair Darling, as secretary of state responsible for transport, admitted that the measure employed by his experts was not 'the best way of measuring congestion' (p. 11). So the studies were about a problem in which the science was contested. The experts applied techniques that were not synchronised with the real world. The Department for Transport conceded that 'it would be better to develop ways of measuring congestion which relate more closely to travellers' experience of delays' (p. 69).

The economic impact

The Commons investigators discovered that the experts had little realistic understanding of the economic impact of transportation. While the CBI had estimated that imperfections in the transport system were costing the economy £20 billion a year, the government's independent adviser, Professor David Begg, acknowledged that their understanding of the true cost of congestion was poor. The Commons committee declared: 'It seems bizarre to plan a strategy around the principle of congestion reduction without having a good understanding of its true costs or long-term impacts' (p. 11).

The financial context

Wishful thinking coloured the government's approach. The consultants disclosed that they were told to search for solutions to the congestion of highways as if there were no financial constraints on the schemes they might propose. They assembled a wish-list of proposals that the transport minister conceded were not affordable. Enter the SRA, which made it clear that it did not regard the studies as the best way to plan a rail network! (p. 53).

Pricing prevarication

The government was open to the idea of charging motorists for access to highways. The transport minister acknowledged that road charging 'is something we need to consider, we need to debate'. The committee was not beguiled: 'But that is more or less the same words that many Secretaries of State have said since the 1960s' (p. 62).

Cost–benefit analysis

Value for money was a litmus test for government. But in examining transport policies, the committee concluded that 'There is no evidence of a cost–benefit analysis of many of the schemes in its Plan' (p. 66). Whitehall's curious approach to forward planning was matched by the operations of the SRA. Priority, in the SRA's view, should be given to its preferred schemes. But the committee revealed that 'There is no evidence of a cost–benefit analysis of many of the schemes in its Plan that would enable it to make this decision' (p. 53). Curtly, it added that the position of the government and the SRA on rail schemes 'does not make sense'.

The planning framework

Even if schemes were shown to be value for money, 'we are extremely concerned that rather than promoting the findings of the studies, recent service cuts may actually undermine the strategies'. In fact, concluded the MPs, far from moving towards an integrated system, the 'planning process is now facing a "disintegrated" implementation process whereby road solutions will dominate because they have committed funding and an effective champion and implementation agency' (p. 67).

Political decision-making

Plans were leading to what the MPs called an 'inevitable outcome' – the further dispersion of people, which would add to severe congestion in the long term (p. 67). Having commissioned the studies on the basis that funding was not a constraint, the Department for Transport found that it could not afford to finance the recommendations (p. 65). The MPs stated the blindingly obvious: 'It is not possible to have a multi-modal programme of improvements if there is no money for rail investment' (p. 66).

Land use

The MPs perceived tensions between land use and transport policies, and they recommended closer liaison between the Department for Transport and the Office of the Deputy Prime Minister, which carried responsibility for land planning (p. 64). The problem was to identify the mechanism for achieving a balance between transport and land use. Was the car, per se, the cause of urban sprawl? That was the opinion of land-use experts, who were commissioned by the Department for Transport to recommend a solution. What they called 'the only effective means of doing so' would be to curtail the use of the car (p. 39, citing Town and Country Planning Association, 1999). But was this putting the cart before the horse? Could the popularity of the car be the consequence of failed policies (cause), rather than urban sprawl (symptom)? If so, might restraints on car ownership be erroneous or premature?

The committee censured the expenditure of large sums of money on consultancy services, and wondered whether this money ought to be spent on infrastructure. Even the secretary of state admitted that the escalating costs of his multi-modal studies were 'frankly unacceptable' (p. 23). The quality of advice did not always appear to justify the cost, in the opinion of the MPs.

Would it be too harsh to accuse government of not knowing whether it was coming or going? The select committee could be forgiven for levelling such an accusation. Five months after informing the committee that it was too early to assess whether the government was going to meet its targets in terms of a *reduction* in congestion, a progress report was published which admitted that congestion would actually *increase* over the ten-year period even if the plan were implemented (p. 13).

How do we account for this depressing assessment of the capabilities of highly paid, dedicated politicians, civil servants and their academic and professional consultants? It appears that no matter how diligent they may be, there was no prospect of delivering an integrated transport plan that was worth the paper on which it was written. One problem was that forecasts were unreliable. Predictions – such as the rate of increase in the purchase of cars or the growth of rail passengers – are derived from assumptions about the rate of growth in GDP and how income affects people's need to travel. Such extrapolations are based on a theory of the business cycle which is not capable of robust forecasts over a period of twelve to eighteen months, let alone a decade.[1]

The outcome is that people are going in circles. Literally. Dr Denvil Coombe, who co-authored the Department for Transport's guidance on the multi-modal studies, and who led the south-west Yorkshire study, said as much. The locations of people's homes and jobs were not sensibly linked to the transport systems. He found that the use of land 'has created a dispersed orbital trip making pattern, which uses unsuitable road network. By its nature, it is also challenging to cater for by public transport'

---

1   Business cycle forecasts are tolerably accurate when the economy is motoring along 'on the flat'; but the empirical evidence shows that people in the economic driving seat tend to be blinkered when they arrive at the bends (see Harrison, 2005).

(House of Commons Transport Select Committee, 2004). One consequence was that people spent more time commuting than their European counterparts: the average British worker devotes 46 minutes each day to travelling to and from work (Commission for Integrated Transport, 2001).

Surrogate signals

If the market economy as it evolved in the nineteenth century failed to deliver the best possible results, it appears that the methodologies of planners are no more successful. We build roads and lay tracks to add value to the wealth of the nation. That wealth includes the benefits from preserving the natural environment and enriching culture, which make communities attractive as living organisms. The investments yield net gains. How do planners assess these net benefits? They count bodies. How many people will use the new facility, how much time will be saved in transit, and what is that additional benefit worth to users?

The technical problem with this body-counting procedure is that the planner cannot sum the value of all the individual preferences of travellers with accuracy. Arbitrary values are employed as substitutes for the real thing – the actions of the users themselves, which speak louder than words. The historical outcome was inconsistent with the market ethos. In the USA, for example, the militarisation of resource allocation has had more influence over transport planning than the economic imperatives of free enterprise. A British transport planner who held senior positions in the Whitehall hierarchy, A. J. Harrison, neatly summarised the association in *The Economics of Transport Appraisal*. He explained how the methodological impulses came together in the planning strategies of the US Department of Defence:

> While these developments were going on in the US Department of Defence, engineers in the field of urban transport were beginning to develop models of transport systems (paralleling the military systems analysis) which have made it possible to consider evaluating all the components of very large investment programmes at one and the same time and to relate them to the wider urban and land use planning context. (Harrison, 1974: 8)

The market approach would have been to log the impact of transport through the prism of land prices. As every estate agent knows (his knowledge is displayed in his advertisements), the land market delivers a robust account of the net effects of (say) a new railway that comes to town, or a bypass highway that steers traffic away from the city high street. As the rents of land rise or fall, so we know whether there is a net gain or loss to a particular location or the neighbourhood, city or nation.

The data collected by armies of statisticians that are deployed to track the movements of the travelling public, whose values they cannot hope to measure with accuracy, are a substitute for the hard facts provided by the travellers. But the way in which the net benefits are crystallised is not some mysterious act of alchemy. A. J. Harrison succinctly described the process. One example was the electrification of a commuting service, which can lead to 'an increase in rental or property values, while values elsewhere fall, reflecting the changes in relative accessibility which have taken place'. This analysis offers insights into the way in which the wheels of fortune turn to deliver an unequal distribution of the benefits:

Existing users of the service will experience a direct gain in the course of the trips they make, but if they decide to move, they will be able to charge incomers a higher price for their houses than previously, up to the limit of the gain in accessibility, and hence, even though they move from the area, they may be able to take with them, in a capital sum, the benefits in terms of reduced travel times which the rail improvement created. Commuters renting property will not be able to do so: the gain in this instance will be experienced by landlords as long as they are able to adjust the rents they charge accordingly. (Ibid.: 58)

This 'direct gain' is the value that the home owner *would have been willing to pay* when those services were originally provided, but which he was not required to pay.[2] This untapped benefit is called 'consumer surplus' (see Box 3). By default, that value is capitalised into the price of land and retained by existing property owners who do not (of course) choose to transfer it to newcomers to the property market.

Why was the value attributable to land not used to evaluate the financial viability of transport projects? There were two reasons. Rents measure the net benefits generated by infrastructure that are distributed in a form that may be cashed at the bank. Rents are part of the market's pricing mechanism. Planners, imbued by the doctrine of 'market failure', preferred their surrogate measures of benefits. The second problem was that the value of land beneath buildings was not separately recorded: there was no reliable database that could be used to assess the impact of

---

2   The purchasers of homes in the future would be charged for the service; but that charge is bolted on to the price of properties when they are sold. The value of the service is paid to vendors, not the providers of the improved transport facility.

Box 3 **Rent and the consumer's surplus**

The concept of consumer surplus describes how some people are willing to pay more for a product or service than its market price.*

Competition levels prices down to marginal costs. This usually means that an enterprise can make a profit from revenue after defraying all its costs. If a prospective customer is willing to pay £2 when the price of the product is £1, he enjoys a 'surplus' of £1. *Good luck to the consumer!* would be most people's response. When that effect is multiplied by a million, the economic implications are dramatic. We may trace the impact all the way down the pricing chain to the point where the 'surplus' is transformed into the rent of land. This may be viewed as the outcome of either of two routes: (1) downward pressure on prices implies an increase in productivity, yielding gains that people can afford to invest in land; (2) monopoly power associated with land means that owners can extract increases in disposable incomes that result from efficiencies in the economy.

There are exceptions. One relates to the collective bargaining power of trade unions. Another relates to non-unionised workers whose scarce skills enable them to command extraordinary remuneration (such as software programmers in the early years of the computer age). Sooner or later, however, these obstacles are eroded, and landowners are ready to claim the net benefits generated by the cost-cutting progress in the economy.

* Although the concept is treated in the standard economic textbooks; of especial relevance is the study by Rana Roy conducted in collaboration with an independent economic expert group under the chairmanship of Professor Chris Nash of ITS, Leeds: *Infrastructure Cost Recovery under Allocatively Efficient Pricing*, UIC/CER Economic Expert Study: Final Report, London, March 1998 (UIC, Paris, September 1998; available at www.landresearchtrust.org).

new investments. For some, the redistributive effect was best left shrouded in mystery.[3]

This was bound to cause problems. Planners resigned themselves to the use of subsidies derived from taxes. This led to analytical contortions, as displayed by the authors of *Regulatory Reform*. They claimed that 'there is no way of generating these funds other than by causing distortions elsewhere in the economy' (Armstrong et al., 1994: 15–16). This was factually incorrect, but the psychological dissonance could be addressed by a logical explanation for ignoring the value of land. In cost–benefit analysis, it is analytically incorrect to add together both the increase in land values *and* the imputed cash benefits of such things as shorter travel times or the elimination of congestion.

> [P]ossible double counting of benefits … arises from the fact that user benefits, as experienced on the transport network, can be transferred to non-users. One of the most important examples of this derives from the close relationship between changes in land values and changes in transport costs … The important point is that while the benefits might in principle be measured by measuring travel benefits or by measuring changes in property values … the two approaches must not be combined. If they are, benefits will be counted twice. (Harrison, 1974: 57–8)

---

3   The European Commission's 1996 Green Paper on transport pricing reviewed the externalised costs (which taxpayers are often called upon to correct with subsidies) but ignored the external benefits (which are privately appropriated): European Commission, *Towards fair and efficient pricing in transport: policy options for internalising the external costs of transport in the European Union*, Luxembourg: Office for Official Publications of the European Communities, 1996. The European Commission subsequently made amends by commissioning research through the European Conference of Ministers of Transport, some results of which are discussed in Chapter 8.

Planners had a choice: they could collect the information from the marketplace, or they could develop a parallel set of data based on questionnaires, stopwatches and their assumptions about human behaviour. In the ideological climate of the 1960s, the market's pricing signals were dismissed in favour of surrogate signals of human behaviour and preferences. So for 40 years investment in infrastructure was at the mercy of political horse-trading (notably in the USA and Japan) or the calculations of planners (notably in the UK).

The calculations of planners rely on leaps of faith disguised by a spurious statistical precision. For example, planning method-ology relies heavily on estimates of the time saved in trips. That time is multiplied by a notional cash value to provide a guide to the presumed benefits of new investment. But whose values are really portrayed in the cost–benefit analysis – the planner's or the passenger's? The links between subjective and objective time are not well understood (Bates et al., 2001; Noland and Polak, 2002; O'Neil et al., 1998; Yarmey, 2000; Yen et al., 2001). At the very least, these estimates would benefit from being cross-checked with data that revealed what people *did* (the additional rents they were willing to pay for a faster train or a decongested road).

Whose money is it anyway?

Are we unduly harsh in our assessment of conventional cost–benefit analysis? Despite the difficulties, is it not a useful tool for comparing projects that are competing for finance when all other conditions are equal? Unfortunately, the *ceteris paribus* get-out clause cannot be invoked in cases that involve the expend-iture of taxpayers' money. For the *redistributive* impact of government policies involves significant uncertainties. Apart from the uncertainties that relate to the losses flowing from the way government raises revenue, there are major uncertainties associated with the leakages that flow from the way government invests people's money.

Taxes on wages and savings are regressive tools for transferring money from people at the bottom end of the income scales (who tend not to own land) to people in the middle and higher income brackets (who tend to own land). This is the process of transforming earned income into windfall wealth via investment in infrastructure. Pound for taxpayer's pound, the discriminatory redistribution of income from the poor to the rich applies equally to all projects.

The problem of uncertainty arises over the allocation of windfall wealth between the owners of land. Two projects may appear similar (say, one-mile-long bypass highways that transfer traffic away from town centres); but the conventional approach to cost–benefit analysis offers no guide as to the distribution of the windfalls. Project A may deliver nearly all the net gains to one or a few people; Project B may distribute the windfall gains in smaller sums to many landowners. Or Project A may hand all the additional value to someone who is already asset rich, Project B to people who are asset poor.

The only way to remove the uncertainty and arbitrariness is to assess the net effect in terms of the prospective increases and decreases in the rental streams of land in the area affected by the investment. But enriching the methodology of transport planning in this way creates a political problem. First, it entails the admission that government tax-and-spend policies are arbitrary and unfair: they diminish the disposable incomes and living standards of low-income taxpayers in favour of enhancing the value of the assets of higher-income landowners. Second, there is the embarrassment of the unequal distribution of windfall gains between landowners. This is a politically explosive cocktail for politicians.

And yet, to enhance the quality of governance and avoid expensive errors, people should insist on this information being made available. By secreting data on land values, government may invest in projects that are both socially and privately unviable. It may do so by 'cooking the books' – by adjusting the values that it assigns to non-financial benefits to arrive at the ratio of benefits to costs that suits it.

But private investors also need the information on the origins, magnitude and distribution of land values. In the past, the absence of this information led people to make investment decisions that wiped out their savings. The absence of this information permits ambiguities (in the definition of rights and obligations) that distorted private markets and public policy.

The investment errors were not confined to the past, however, as investors in the denationalised British Rail would affirm. More than 200,000 of them bought shares in Railtrack. They thought there was clarity over the finances associated with the company. In fact, the information void allowed ambiguities and errors to flourish. These sealed the fate of Railtrack and led 45,000 shareholders to sue the Secretary of State for Transport. Although the case was not presented in our terms, at the heart of the High Court drama was the unresolved problem of the rights to, and responsibilities of, the value that was created by the railway.[4]

---

4   Comprehensive reports on the High Court proceedings appeared in the *Daily Telegraph*, beginning with the issue of 28 June 2005.

- Investors purchased Railtrack shares at £3.80 in the belief that taxpayers would continue to subsidise the network. At their peak (in 1998) shares reached £17.68.
- In 1999 and 2000, two train crashes claimed 35 lives. Attention was drawn to past under-investment. Someone had to pay to upgrade the tracks and signalling systems. Share prices tumbled.
- Government grew anxious about the political fall-out. Travellers and trade unions criticised as anomalous the payment of dividends while taxpayers subsidised the infrastructure.

Shareholders believed that they were entitled to dividends from the money they entrusted to Railtrack, but the company also needed taxpayers' cash to fund capital improvements. This economic reality was a public relations disaster for a Labour government that tried to live with a privatised rail system. The government was confronted with what was perceived as a funding quandary. The Treasury and the Department for Transport decided to tip Railtrack into administration on the grounds that it was bankrupt. Was it? Wasn't Railtrack creating enough value to cover all its costs, including the tracks and stations? The shareholders who sued the former Secretary of State for Transport implicitly thought so. They *expected* government to fund the infrastructure out of taxpayers' money, because that was customary. Would the contradictions and ambiguities in people's perceptions have arisen if there was clarity over the origins, rights and responsibilities of the value that leaked out of the railways and into the pockets of landowners?

A resolution of the financial and fiscal issues that underpin disputes of the Railtrack kind is needed as the prelude to rebuilding institutions and the laws that determine rights and responsibilities. But an informed debate cannot occur in an informational vacuum. Reforms are resisted until people can judge how their private and social interests would be affected. Above all, in our view, they need data on the magnitude and distribution of rent. Rent, as determined by people through their everyday transactions, is a barometer of efficiency and fairness. As such, it enhances the democratic principles of transparency and account-ability, by exposing impacts that governments strive to conceal. Rent is an independent audit of the quality of governance, as well as the productivity of the economy.

The rent barometer

Viewed historically, the nationalisation of Britain's private enter-prises and the resort to centralised planning was the result, ulti-mately, of the failure to employ rent as the principal economic guide to public policy. We shall test this proposition in Chapters 6 and 7 by scrutinising the twists and turns of events in the evolu-tion of transport systems. Modern transportation may be dated from the decision of the 3rd Duke of Bridgewater to construct a canal (1761–65). The canal transformed the coal seams beneath his agricultural acres into streams of liquid gold, by boosting the rent rolls of his estate in the north of England. Canals made it possible to slash the cost of coal in the markets. Thus, they became vehicles for securitising, and transferring ownership over, future streams of rent.

The fragile nature of the financial system that supported this revolution surfaced in the 'mania' that exploded between 1791 and 1794. Speculation in the shares of new projects lured investors into ruin. The fortunes that nourished the psychology of speculation were reaped by landowners, not shareholders.

The days of the canal were numbered when they succumbed to the temptations of monopoly power.

> Canals prospered and became finally characterised by all the abuses inseparable from prosperous monopolies. Prosperity brought stereotyped rigidity and petrifaction. The owning companies were finally more concerned to maintain and increase their own profits than to meet the growing requirements of commerce, and from that period (the early part of the 19th century) dates their downfall. (Kirkaldy and Evans, 1931: 25)

Similar problems awaited the railways, which meant that they were ill equipped to deal with the challenge presented by Henry Ford's mass production of automobiles. And similar crises exist today, this time with taxpayers as the 'shareholders' who will continue to lose fortunes if there is no revision to the fiscal and financial architecture that frames the economy. But fundamental reform entails a challenge to cherished beliefs.

New approaches to public finance may be the pre-condition for improvements to the services delivered by transportation. Such issues, however, cannot be viewed in isolation from the general problem of the quality of governance. That there is widespread disaffection with government is not contested. At the heart of the dissatisfaction is discontent with the way government raises revenue and the efficiency with which it delivers its services. The quality and impact of tax policy, then, ought to be at the heart of the debate about the choices made by government on behalf of the people. But as A. J. Harrison (1974: 150) acknowledged, in relation to transport policy: 'The standard treatment of taxation in economic appraisal is to ignore it.'

If government is to be held accountable we cannot ignore the impact of fiscal policy. New yardsticks are needed to test the efficiency with which taxpayers' money is disbursed. Adam Smith identified the rent of land – as a source of public revenue – as setting the standard for the performance of tax policy: 'Every tax ought to be so contrived as both to take out and to keep out of the pockets of the people as little as possible, over and above what it brings into the treasury of the state' (Smith, 1776 [1981]: 826).

By this test, taxes ought not to inflict losses on people who work, save and invest. That this principle of good governance is routinely abused is beyond dispute. But it is not just taxes which cause losses. Because the state now penetrates all levels of the economy, it has acquired enormous powers of regulation. In Britain, the regulations that are deemed to be 'bad' are estimated to cost firms a sum that exceeds the £118 billion raised by income tax (2003/04). This is a dead loss for enterprises that survive by holding down their costs of production.[5]

Economists agree that there is one source of revenue only which meets Smith's test of good governance. This is how one of the world's best-selling university teaching manuals puts it:

> [A] tax on rent will lead to no distortions or economic inefficiencies. Why not? Because a tax on pure economic rent does not change anyone's economic behaviour ... hence, the economy operates after the tax exactly as it did before the tax – with no distortions or inefficiencies arising as a result of the tax. (Samuelson and Nordhaus, 1985: 605; emphasis in original)

---

5 The estimate is by Sir David Arculus, chairman of the Blair government's Better Regulation Task Force, cited in Moules (2005).

Is it possible to view rents as the basis of a new approach to providing transport systems on the back of free enterprise rather than the pockets of taxpayers? Paul Reichmann, a Canadian entrepreneur, thought he could initiate such a reform. He did not reckon with the artfulness of the modern bureaucracy.

3   FREE TRAINS OR FREE RIDERS?

Reichmann's windfall train

Paul Reichmann had a dream. He and his brothers would challenge the oldest banking district in the world by building a financial centre on wasteland in the heart of London. They would compete with the City by offering the great financial houses accommodation in purpose-built skyscrapers. They had money aplenty including the biggest property empire in North America, which had amassed assets of $25 billion. Ingenuity was no problem: they had accomplished feats where other entrepreneurs had feared to tread. Had they not built the World Financial Centre on a sandbar in New York's Hudson River? Daring was a family characteristic: in their youth, as Hitler tried to conquer Europe, from their enclave in Tangier they worked to defy the Nazis, launching covert mercy missions to keep alive the victims of the concentration camps.

But without good transport links, their dream was not viable.

Shrewdly, they acquired an 80-acre site on the Isle of Dogs in what was once the heart of a transport hub that knitted together a seafaring empire. The Reichmanns were offered a good deal by the government. Prime Minister Margaret Thatcher, in her bid to regenerate the area, turned Docklands into an enterprise zone. The brothers would be relieved of taxes on rents earned by their company, Olympia & York (O&Y). Here, out of the derelict docks, they could construct a masterpiece that combined the finest architecture with commercial vitality. They would lure the financiers from their mansions in the stockbroker belt to create a real estate for the 21st century. The government's Development Corporation promised to build new roads and, critically, to extend the as yet unopened Docklands Light Railway. The Reichmanns agreed to contribute half the estimated £130 million cost of the extension.

But they soon discovered two flaws in their plan. The light railway had not been designed to carry the traffic volumes that would be required to serve their estate. Even more critical, however, was the realisation that a link into the City was not enough to lure the major tenants. Staff would have to travel first into the old centre of London, then back out to their Canary Wharf. A new line was needed to cut journey times.

The brothers believed they were dealing with a government that understood market economics. But they were reluctant to place their project at the mercy of the bureaucracy. If they needed a train, they would provide one for themselves. They did their sums. They could construct an underground railway that would link the Waterloo and London Bridge commuter rail terminals with Canary Wharf. The line would run eastwards from the rail hubs south of the river, dip under the Thames and deliver in style the lawyers, journalists and bankers whose firms would relocate in their skyscrapers. Based on costs of new railways in other cities, O&Y and its advisers calculated that they could build the railway for £400–600 million.

The numbers were encouraging. With just the light railway – once it was made to work – O&Y could expect to get £20 per square foot per year, enough to cover their costs and make a modest profit. With an efficient rail system linking Waterloo and London Bridge, O&Y could charge something nearer to the £55–60 a square foot that bankers paid for space in the City.[1] This suggested an increase in annual rents of about £30 a square foot. With plans to build more than 10 million square feet of space, they could expect additional annual rental income of more than £320 million. At a 10 per cent discount rate that represented a capital sum of £3.2 billion.

Paul Reichmann took the lead. He recognised that, if all went well, he could recover the cost of the underground line in just two years. But he was walking into two traps. The first was the cycle in the property market. This was rapidly heading for a peak just as O&Y was laying the foundations for its prestigious glass-and-marble buildings. O&Y was to fall victim on a heroic scale. With debts running into billions of pounds, as Britain went into recession in the early 1990s the Reichmanns were driven back to North America by a debt burden that broke records. The second obstacle was the capacity of Britain's bureaucracy to run a guer-rilla campaign in favour of the ethos of state control.

The Reichmanns were misled by the propaganda – that the Thatcher government was dedicated to market-based reforms. The problem was not with Margaret Thatcher herself, whose political instincts matched the Reichmanns' financial philosophy. The prime minister had encouraged her ministers to explore new ways of funding infrastructure without loading the cost on to taxpayers. Who, after all, was going to pocket the net gains from a new underground line to Canary Wharf? Why should taxpayers,

---

1   'London Docklands: where derelict land is a greenfield site', *The Economist*, 13 February 1988.

most of whom would never ride the new line, pay for it when the railway could be financed by billionaire property moguls?

Paul Channon was Thatcher's cabinet minister in charge of transport. He had no hesitation in declaring that the people who benefited would have to pay: 'The Government believes that, if there is to be new investment in transport in London, the passengers who will benefit, should meet the cost of it through the fares they pay, rather than be subsidised by taxpayers in the rest of the country' (Channon, 1989). But the fares paid by passengers would not be sufficient to cover the capital investment in acquiring land, digging the tunnels and laying the tracks. Who would fund the infrastructure? Channon declared: 'Contributions should also be forthcoming from property owners and developers who stand to gain from the improvements to transport' (ibid.).

This was a radical departure from conventional fiscal philosophy. The new doctrine would accomplish two things. First, there would be symmetry between the payments and those who enjoyed the benefits. This was the application of the principle to which we all conform, in the rest of our lives: *paying for the benefits that we receive*. If landowners were going to make money from a new gravy train, why should they not fund it? Second, the idea that 'public' services could – should – be defrayed out of the value of land was a renewal of conservatism in the literal, historical sense. Traditionally, from the earliest civilisations onwards, the services that people shared were financed out of their economy's surplus. This surplus surfaced as the rents that people were willing to pay for the use of land and the resources of nature. That age-old principle had been sidetracked by the revolutionaries of Europe in the late feudal era – the aristocracy – but Thatcher appeared to be excavating the fiscal doctrine for a post-socialist Britain.

The philosophy was precisely stated in a Department of Transport study that was commissioned to examine competing railway projects. London Underground had long cherished a Tube line – called Crossrail – that linked the overland stations at Paddington with Liverpool Street. Should this have priority over Reichmann's line? The question was complicated by a difference over the route that the second Tube line would take. O&Y defined their preferred route, and called it the Waterloo & Greenwich Railway. The transport planners at London Underground toyed with the variations, and they called the O&Y route the Jubilee Line Extension. Whichever project was chosen, there was no doubt about who should pay:

> The evaluation of options has been conducted within the framework provided by the Government's policy on the financing of rail services. This requires that any new line should be paid for by those who benefit including passengers, property developers and landowners … In the case of the Extension to the Jubilee Line we understand that the Department of Transport has been advised that the *benefits which the line would bring to property developers and landowners are likely to exceed by a substantial margin the cost of the line*, and that a Government contribution to the funding would not appear to be needed. (Halcrow Fox & Associates, 1989: 31; emphasis added)

O&Y endorsed this financial philosophy. Employees already paid the cost of commuting from their homes beyond the green belt; and, suggested O&Y, they would be willing to pay a premium for an efficient, comfortable Tube line that swiftly carried them to their offices every morning. The fare box would collect enough money to cover the operating costs of the trains. As for the capital costs – O&Y was willing to fund the construction of a Tube line that would enhance the value of their real estate.

Paul Reichmann was willing to foot the bill. London Underground would receive – as a gift – a valuable piece of infrastructure that would serve the residents of the capital for generations. No one in living memory could recall such generosity. Mishandling by the government and the transport bureaucracy allowed that gift to slip from the nation's hands.

Turf wars

The obstacles placed in the way of O&Y began with a dispute over the cost of constructing the Tube line. This was estimated by a transport specialist whom the Reichmanns hired from Toronto, their home city in Canada.

Michael Schabas had learnt his transport economics at Harvard's Kennedy School of Government. He then worked on the Vancouver rapid transit system, and was working in Hawaii when he read *The Economist* article that called Paul Reichmann Mr Big. O&Y were doing their sums, and they indicated that they would need a new transport facility. Schabas was hired by O&Y. The Waterloo & Greenwich Railway could be built at a cost of between £400 million and £600 million, estimated O&Y. London Transport rejected the estimate: their experts said it would cost £800 million.

The rule for private enterprise is that when the money is coming out of your pocket you avoid waste: you opt for the deal that is efficient. O&Y did not expect to receive taxpayers' money, so it developed costings in the knowledge that a penny saved was a penny more in profits. But the planners claimed to know better. Schabas was challenged to prove that private enterprise could deliver the Tube line at a lower cost than the public sector. He drew up the specifications and circulated them to five eminent engineering and construction corporations, including Trafalgar House, Mowlem, Taylor Woodrow and Balfour Beatty. Their estimates ranged between £480 million and £600 million. The most competitive quote was £300 million less than London Transport expected to pay. Schabas (1994: 17) recalls that 'dealing directly with contractors, suggesting that London Transport had no monopoly on railway building skills, was seen as a particular affront and won us few friends at 55 Broadway [HQ of London Transport]'.

The next challenge was the time that it would take to prepare a Bill to submit to Parliament for powers to acquire the land. London Transport said it would take a full year – and that the application would have to go through them. O&Y put together a team which prepared a Bill within three months.

The O&Y empire was not built on a propensity to waste resources. It had expanded, building by building across the United States and Canada, with acute attention to detail – and the willingness to work fast. And Paul Reichmann believed that the Thatcher doctrine of private enterprise equipped the government for the ways of the businessman. He was wrong, as he discovered when the day came to negotiate how much O&Y would pay for the new railway.

The cash offer was hand-delivered by Michael Schabas in the late summer of 1988. The outcome was revealed to O&Y executives at their offices in Great George Street. Michael Schabas recalls:

> Paul Reichmann's opening offer was to pay two-thirds of

the capital cost of the railway. London Underground said 'No!' Paul told us that he was willing to pay the full sum, and hand them the tube line – but we would want to participate in the management of the construction work. Two-thirds was meant to be the opening offer. London Underground needed to go back to Paul with a counter-offer. He waited for them to do so. He had done his sums. He knew that the tube would make it possible for him to charge an additional £30 for every square foot of rentable space. That meant he could recover the capital cost of the railway in two years. But London Underground did not come back to him. They didn't even try to negotiate – they hoped he would just go away.[2]

The moment was lost. The politicians prevaricated. The planners at London Transport preferred to promote Crossrail. The O&Y team read the sub-text. The capitalist developers – and foreigners at that – were upstarts who had no right to interfere with railways, which were in the public domain.

O&Y's attempt to fund and build a railway was an embarrassment for the planners. Margaret Thatcher was furious and insisted they could not just turn away Reichmann's offer. The traditional political escape route was followed: set up another study. That was the fate that befell the Waterloo & Greenwich Railway. The Department of Transport, having commissioned the *Central London Rail Study* (January 1989), then commissioned *The East London Rail Study* (September 1989). As if that did not provide sufficient information to make an informed judgement on what was required to keep the wheels of fortune turning in the London metropolis, the Treasury joined the transport

2 Michael Schabas, interview, 22 January 2004.

agencies to produce a third report in 1990. What was the value of this study to the decision-makers? It purported to compare the costs and benefits of the railway options, employing the London Transport Study Model. This was a 'multi-modal model' (Department of Transport et al., 1990: 19). But the planners' analytical tools excluded:

- environmental costs and benefits;
- savings from fewer road accidents;
- benefits from urban regeneration;
- the value of more jobs in the financial centre and the heightened attractions of London for tourists;
- reduced delays for passengers on the Underground, including the elimination of the need to close 50 stations that had already become dangerously overcrowded during peak travel times.

Were these omissions bizarre, or were they acceptable for decision-making agencies whose responsibility included the environment, public safety, urban renewal, employment and the efficient operation of the rail network? Did the methodology suggest a desire to evaluate projects comprehensively; or an introverted fixation with purely transport-related considerations?

Missing from the official studies was the vision brought to the task of enriching the London economy by enterprises such as O&Y.

O&Y kept close to the East London Rail Study team, to make sure it did not bury their proposals. The Waterloo & Greenwich Railway metamorphosed into the Jubilee Line Extension, a much bigger scheme serving many areas besides Canary Wharf. The costs would be higher because of the plan to connect into the existing Jubilee Line. For London Underground, the Jubilee Line was unfinished business, although the route would have to be changed to serve Canary Wharf.

Although the East London Rail Study (ELRS) would not be published until late 1989, O&Y would not wait. During the summer, it again funded a joint team with London Underground to prepare the necessary legislation, which was deposited with Parliament for the October 1989 deadline. The path through Parliament was now tortuous, however, at least partly because of changes suggested by the planners.

Simon Hughes, the MP through whose constituency the Tube line would pass, wanted stations to be built in Southwark and Bermondsey. The ELRS had suggested these, but the benefits did not match the costs. Hughes promoted the interests of his constituents. He filibustered the Bill. Were the additional stations necessary, and who would pay? Now anxious not to delay the scheme, the Department of Transport recomputed the costs and benefits and reported their findings to Norman Lamont, Chief Secretary to the Treasury. The Bermondsey station, in an area where the land was largely in public ownership, with a heavy incidence of public housing, would cost an additional £23 million, and the benefits exceeded the costs by a ratio of 1.34:1. The Southwark station, if it included an interchange link to Waterloo, would cost £39 million, with benefits exceeding costs by a ratio of 2.99:1.[3] The Jubilee Line's cost escalated, but it appeared that the investment would be worthwhile. There was, however, one little problem: the capital costs could not be covered by the fares from passengers. And O&Y

3   Roger Freeman, 'Jubilee Line extension: Southwark and Bermondsey', letter, Department of Transport, 27 September 1990.

saw no reason why it should foot the inflated bill out of the rents of Canary Wharf.

Simon Hughes argued that the stations would help to regenerate an area that had been neglected. But as for who would pay, there was little doubt: the costs would fall on the nation's taxpayers rather than those who would directly benefit, the residents and businesses in the constituency where the net gains would cascade once the wheels were rolling.

Taxpayers were to foot a bill of £3.4 billion. *The cost was approximately equal to the total uplift in value which the Reichmanns had anticipated for their land alone!*

O&Y commissioned an assessment of what its portion of the total benefits would be. This concluded that the project sponsored by the public sector had overestimated the costs and underestimated the benefits. Crucially, O&Y was not the only estate that would benefit.

> [T]he benefits to landowners are not concentrated in such as
> [*sic*] way that they form an easily identifiable tax base. The
> gains to property owners arising from a rail link adding to
> an existing large network, as the Jubilee Line extension does,
> will be very diffuse. It is for this reason that the Government
> decided it could not attempt to collect contributions from
> landowners and developers benefiting from the East West
> Crossrail. (Jones Lang Wootton, 1989: viii)

The O&Y critique explored the consequences of increasing the cost of the line from £277 million (if the line were confined to serving O&Y's interests) to the cost that would satisfy the interests of a wider constituency. The Treasury had failed to catch up with the government's fiscal philosophy. It had not suggested a mechanism to enable landowners in Southwark to defray the cost of a new station. Would the landowners have done so to enjoy an increase in the value of their land? One property restorer in the area, Don Riley, would have been amenable. He has since recorded how the properties he manages appreciated as a result of the arrival of the Jubilee Line (Riley, 2001).

O&Y calculated that, in terms of the total uplift in land values, 'Canary Wharf is likely to experience no more than 19 per cent of the betterment, but were Olympia and York to pay 19 per cent of any contribution to the cost of constructing the line, they would, in effect, be subsidising other landowners and developers' (ibid.: x). Why should O&Y *volunteer* to share the capital costs of a railway with taxpayers, enabling other landowners to enjoy a free ride? In the event, it did contribute £100 million.

A four-year episode that did not reflect glory on the politicians and planners ended. As Schabas was to ruefully reflect:

> In retrospect, it was tragic that O&Y's original offer was turned down. Even had O&Y still gone bust, London would have got a new tube line for a fraction of the final price. Private involvement would certainly have speeded the project along and helped keep costs under control. But without support from London Transport's leadership, and without some sort of competitive price check, Government officials lacked the confidence that it could defend O&Y's offer as a good deal. (Schabas, 1994:18)

Despite the Thatcher government's stress on the need for beneficiaries to pay, the new fiscal philosophy had not percolated down to the civil servants. The Jubilee Line was financed in a way that delivered riches to many free riders, at the expense of taxpayers.[4]

Dividing the spoils

How to share the spoils that flow from an improvement in transport did not feature in political discourse until the arrival of the Reichmann brothers.

In relation to the Jubilee Line, the government was left in no doubt that the 'funding gap'[5] could be bridged by the anticipated increases in the rental income that would flow to the owners of land. These rents reflected the enhanced economic opportunities, which were not overlooked by entrepreneurs like O&Y. Schabas identified some prospects when he walked the route of his proposed Waterloo & Greenwich Railway. He reported to Reichmann that many choice sites were ripe for redevelopment. Reichmann replied: 'That's interesting. How secret can we keep this?' Scouts were sent to evaluate land in the vicinity of the proposed stations. Land values, the Reichmanns knew, would rise. But this was not the outcome of a mysterious process. The economics were well understood by North American transport experts. Schabas explains:

---

4   In March 2004, London's Traffic Commissioner, Bob Kiley, reported that a study commissioned by Transport for London from Jones Lang LaSalle estimated that the uplift in land values as a result of the influence of the Jubilee Line was in the order of £2 billion at Canary Wharf and £800 million around the Southwark station. A parallel study by Atis Real Weatherall reported an uplift in property values of a similar magnitude around these two stations. Both reports are available on the Transport for London website (www.tfl.gov.uk).

5   The difference between the present value of the revenues, and the capital and operating costs.

If you don't charge commuters for the benefits of the
new train service, and if there are other benefits – such
as reductions in congestion, or improvements to the
environment – these are captured by the owners of the land
through which people travel. Congestion relief benefits
accrue to those who own homes and offices. In that respect,
Canary Wharf and its major tenants capture many of the
benefits of the Jubilee Line, because they do not have to pay
staff quite as much as they would if access to the Isle of Dogs
was more difficult.[6]

O&Y would not be the only property company to appropriate
the increase in land values. For the principle that was promoted
by the government – that the windfall gains to landowners could
be used to finance the infrastructure – was not converted into
practical solutions. As Schabas noted: 'Nobody came up with a
good idea as to how to capture any of this, with two exceptions.'
First, the government did not hesitate 'to hold O&Y to ransom …
stat[ing] that unless £600 million was forthcoming the line would
not be built'. The Reichmanns were veterans at the game of bluff;
the government was the first to flinch. O&Y did agree to pay £400
million, but only £100 million was up front. The remainder would
be paid over many years. Discounted at the government's 6 per
cent cost of borrowing money, the contribution was worth something closer to £150 million.

The second device, suggested by Schabas, was an auction to
determine the course of the Jubilee Line along one section of the
route just east of Canary Wharf. The East London Rail Study had
considered two alternatives, running either via the Greenwich

6   Interview, 22 January 2004.

Peninsula or Leamouth. The Leamouth site was already being developed, and would be served with another branch of the light railway. It was also in fragmented ownership. British Gas, which owned virtually the entire Greenwich Peninsula, won with an offer reputed to be worth £25 million, but part of which was apparently given as land rather than cash (Schabas, 1994: 18). The Jubilee Line trains were routed beneath the Greenwich Peninsula, on which the infamous Millennium Dome was later to be built.

Crossrail remained a dream: the money could not be found. Brian Wilson, MP, speaking at the second reading of the Crossrail Bill on 8 June 1993, declared: 'In respect of Crossrail, we still do not know where the money will come from … That is a strange way to plan the transport needs of our country for the next century.'

As the planners dreamed, overcrowding on the trains was matched by congestion on the roads. The inefficient circulation of people imposed constraints on the productivity of the London economy. In the early years of the 21st century, government agencies were still arguing with a private sector consortium over who should pay for Crossrail. Another Bill was submitted to Parliament in 2005 to authorise its construction, but there was no agreement on where the funding would come from.

The free riders

The controversial origins of the Jubilee Line Extension (JLE) help us to identify fundamental problems associated with the way transport services are created and delivered.

On the funding of infrastructure, the conventional wisdom is simplistic. Either the money is available from the taxpayer, or it is not. This reduces the financial challenge to a political conundrum.

Margaret Thatcher proved to be more imaginative. She proposed to apply the principle that beneficiaries ought to defray the capital costs. Her initiative failed.

O&Y, as a landowner, could capture some of the additional value that was created by the infrastructure. This value is 'externalised', in the sense that – in a competitive market – it cannot be captured in freight charges and passenger fares. Eurotunnel, for example, unlike O&Y, does not have the commercial scope for 'internalising' some of the rental value which the Channel Tunnel creates. The rents are diffused throughout Britain. Private enterprises that do not also operate as property companies do not have the power to claw back some of the additional value they help to create. For them to do so, they need the cooperation of an enlightened taxing authority.

Did the problem illustrated by Eurotunnel originate in doctrinal confusion over the ownership of the spatial terrain within which our communities are located? Private property rights are exercised, but the state reserves eminent domain unto itself – and it has secured ultimate control over the *use* of land through the planning laws. Has this splitting of rights led to conflicts that distract people from the most efficient uses to which they could put land? This question cannot be sensibly answered until we perceive space as something more than traversable land.

Land is assigned value which may vary considerably over short distances. If there are competing claims over the ownership and use of that value, might this account for the decisions which, on occasion, appear to undermine people's individual and shared interests? Might these conflicting claims account for the absence of symmetry in the distribution of costs and benefits? Might the costs associated with investments on, and use of, space be imposed on one group of people, while the benefits accrue to others? If such an incongruous dynamic is at work, it would be especially evident in transportation, the lattice-work that binds the spatial framework of communities.

Unfortunately, planners employ economic concepts that disguise the consequences arising from investment. Their cost–benefit analyses are framed within the neo-classical model. This treats the economy as two-dimensional, composed of labour and capital (Bannister, 1994: 52). Land is conflated into 'capital'. So for analytical purposes, transport planners denied themselves a comprehensive appreciation of how roads and railways are located in the larger spatial context. That space is an *economic* space, as well as the framework that could be visualised in engineering, or environmental, terms. This was a fatal deterioration in the planner's methodology. For land's *value* is the bridge between space as a biospherical entity and the social reality of civilisation. Transit systems integrate that space, helping to fructify the relationship between a community and its natural environment. Might the failure to incorporate the value of land into transport models account for grievous errors in policy?

Among the issues raised by the Docklands episode is the value-for-money principle. The Blair government think tank on transport, the Commission for Integrated Transport, noted that 'there is evidence of "gold plating" of some UK transport projects to include elements that go beyond the functional (stations on the JLE extension) or for specification of additional, expensive capabilities at the design stage of a project which may be of limited subsequent value. Good design does not have to carry a high price tag' (Commission for Integrated Transport, 2004). The Commission cited staff costs (project management, planning, design and legal issues) which were estimated as 25 per cent of scheme costs in the UK compared with 3 per cent of costs for Spain's Madrid–Lerida Line.

The Commission also highlighted the cost of land, which appeared to be greater than in other countries. But is the high cost of land a problem or, as O&Y represented it, a solution? Within the current funding paradigm, it does indeed appear to be an obstacle. But might it be possible to recalibrate that model to convert the land market into part of the solution?

The need for a radical reappraisal is suggested by the Commission's finding that, if Britain adopted more efficient procedures to finance railways, cost savings of about 20–30 per cent should be possible. This would make a high-speed rail network of the kind enjoyed on the Continent financially feasible. But this would entail changes to processes that are currently cherished by the transport planners. Not least, there are problems with planning procedures, the delays from which increase costs of projects such as the modernisation of the rail network (ibid.: para. 13).

We need to contest assumptions about the interface between the public and private sectors. The Reichmanns were willing to invest their private resources in 'public' services because they appreciated the economic benefits of infrastructure to landowners. If the investment is viable the benefits are diffused *and landowners receive the net gains as increases in land values*. Can this economic process be adapted to resolve problems with investment in transport?

Planners believe that 'the private sector cannot replace the public sector for capital investment in the *infrastructure*, [so] there must be some form of partnership' (Bannister, 1994: 81). This view depends on the way the economic gains from investments are distributed. We shall see that planners (both private consultants and civil servants), on the strength of the information they gather, are not qualified to offer such a dogmatic verdict. O&Y's railway is a metaphor for what may be offered by the private sector, through market economics: a railway that is free to the public, funded by those who benefit from its construction. The alternative is the Jubilee Line, in which the owners of land enjoy free rides on the backs of taxpayers.

But free riders are only a symptom of the general problem of the way in which we use and abuse rent. Can rents be turned from a problem into the solution? Do institutional solutions exist outside the framework of direct government ownership and control? For some answers, we need to travel to the Far East.

4 FAR EASTERN PROMISES

Infrascapes

Infrastructure reconfigures the landscape, economy and society. Capital is aggregated on such a massive scale (think of motorways) that it has the power literally to move mountains. Projects may involve profound social commitments (think of nuclear power stations) such that, if errors are made, freedoms of whole populations may be compromised. The farther removed our lives are from the state of nature, the deeper our reliance on the fabric of the built environment, the component parts of which are bonded together by the services delivered by the infrastructure. Nowhere is this dynamic process more evident than in the great metropolises that are exploding on the surface of the globe.

> It so happens that railway stations, airports, motorway service stations and even toll booths are becoming the incubators of a whole new urban experience. Not only are the forms of public space changing, but new models of social behaviour and use of time are also developing. These indirectly reflect upon the way the external city is experienced and utilised. (Clementi, 2003: 41)

If policy errors are to be avoided by the growth centres of the 21st century, a deeper appreciation of optimal financial strategies will be needed. Fortunately, we are not embarking into the unknown. A glimpse of the future may be gleaned from a look into the past. Valuable lessons may be derived from Hong Kong, Singapore and Japan, where the combination of transport and property policies served as the catalyst for flourishing communities.

- The tax burden in Hong Kong and Singapore is exceedingly low compared with the UK and USA (see Table 3). The important point, however, is *not* the absolute level of tax take, but *how* the revenue is raised; which in the case of Hong Kong and Singapore is biased in favour of rents. This implies that the UK and USA would generate higher per capita incomes if they enjoyed a similarly low tax burden complemented by rental revenue raised direct from what people are willing to pay to use public spaces.
- All three Far Eastern countries are resource poor, but they deliver incomes and productivity levels equal to, or much higher than, countries that are rich in natural resources. If the territories of Hong Kong and Singapore were endowed with domestic sources of petroleum and precious metals, they would outperform the USA in terms of per capita incomes.

The Far Eastern countries are densely populated: they cannot afford to waste space. The market-based tools they developed to deal with that pressure are revealing. Hong Kong and Singapore are rated at the top of the most comprehensive Index of Economic Freedom. Japan's record is also not contested: she came from nowhere after World War II to create the second-largest economy in the world. Comparing their transport policies with those of the UK and USA may help to sharpen the insights

Table 3 **Vital statistics of selected countries (comparative data (2002) based on the Index of Economic Freedom)**

	Hong Kong	Singapore	Japan	UK	USA
Rank	1	2	35	9	6
Fiscal burden	2	2	4	4	3.5
Income tax rates:					
Top rate	17	22	37	40	39.1
Marginal rate (average payer)	17	8	20	22	27.5
Corporation tax: per cent	16	22	30	30	35
Government expenditure: per cent GDP	21.6	18.1	36.9	38.3	30.4
GDP per capita: $	24,506	26,806	43,042	22,241	31,932
Population (million)	6.7	4.1	127.3	59.8	284.7
Total area (000 sq. km)	1	0.647	377	244	9,629
People per sq. km	6,700	6,384	337	245	29

Source: Heritage Foundation (2003)

that have emerged in this study. We focus our analysis in terms of three hypotheses.

Hypothesis I: Taxpayer subsidies are an inevitable part of mass transit systems

The durability of this assumption was affirmed by the spokesman for Britain's Strategic Rail Authority. David Thomas (2003) claimed that there are only two types of income for rail projects: fares and subsidy. The demand for subsidies is rationalised by a political vocabulary that presupposes the inability of railways to pay their way. The collateral damage of this doctrine to the fabric of political institutions is significant. If subsidies are to be extracted from taxpayers and transferred to railways, government has the right to control the industry.

One consequence is the touting of solutions that are self-defeating. Take the case of the need to increase fares to pay for infrastructure. This proposition was advanced by Richard Bowker as chairman of the SRA. He argued that upkeep of the rail network rests too heavily on taxpayers and that 'passengers should pay more' (Bream, 2004). To raise fares closer to the actual cost of rail travel would be likely to price more passengers off the railway. This would render rail companies even less able to cover their operating costs, let alone the costs of capital, and consequently increase the demand for more subsidies.

Hong Kong (see p. 87) rejects the subsidy mentality. Is this the product of a philosophy of public finance that does not favour taxes that deliver deadweight losses?

Hypothesis II: Road prices are unaffordable and regressive

Roads are a precious finite asset. If we charged rents for the use of that space, would we prejudice the mobility needs of people at the lower end of the income scales? This is one of the fears aroused by the proposal to introduce nationwide road pricing in Britain.

Singapore (see p. 94) favours the road charging philosophy. The very high rents that are voluntarily paid for road space are used to hold down taxes and to fund a high-quality transit system that is available to everybody. Has this policy contributed to the per capita GDP incomes that exceed Britain's?

Hypothesis III: Efficient railways are those in public ownership

The House of Commons Treasury Committee, after reviewing a decade's worth of evidence in running privatised railways, endorsed this view in *The Future of the Railway*. The view was shared by the head of the Rail, Maritime and Transport Union, who claimed that rail privatisation was 'an act of vandalism that tore apart our national railway network and handed it in 113 pieces to the private sector to bleed dry' (Crow, 2003). In the British circumstances, there was force to his claim that separating the ownership of tracks from the operation of the trains 'would be an act of dangerous folly – and that the only way profits would be made by the private sector was by taxpayers and passengers subsidising them' (ibid.).

But had the nationalised British Rail (BR) been a paragon of operational efficiency? Transport Minister Kim Howells told the House of Commons Transport Committee that BR had been 'an appalling service'. It had employed some managers who were 'rubbish'. An eight-year-old child could have come up with better cost estimates than those managers, he asserted.[1]

Japan's railways (see p. 97) may provide evidence to help us resolve some of the contentious issues. Her rail network is a rich mixture of public and private enterprises, and the latter have not prejudiced the ability of the Japanese to operate an efficient economy.

Hong Kong: a colonial legacy

The colonial roots of Hong Kong's financial system are revealing. The toehold on China was to be one of the British Empire's transport hubs. The terms on which the colony would be administered were dispatched from the Foreign Office on

---

1   'Rail safety too pricey – minister', *Guardian*, 6 November 2003.

4 January 1843. Lord Aberdeen, the Foreign Secretary, was explicit:

> The principal source from which revenue is to be looked for is the Land; and if by the liberality of the Commercial regulations enforced in the Island, foreigners as well as British Subjects are tempted to establish themselves on it, and thus to make it a great mercantile Entrepôt, with very limited dimensions, Her Majesty's Government conceived that they would be fully justified in securing to the Crown all the benefits to be expected from the increased value which such a state of things would confer upon Land. Her Majesty's Government would therefore caution you against the permanent alienation of any portion of the land, and they would prefer that Parties should hold land under Leases from the Crown, the terms of which might be sufficiently long to warrant the holders in building upon their allotments ... It would probably be advantageous also that the portions of land should be let by auction. (Welsh, 1997: 149)

This philosophy integrated public finance with private property rights. It transformed a sterile outcrop on the edge of China into the most dynamic of capitalist economies. If we need a living example of Adam Smith's model of the enterprise economy, Hong Kong met the specifications. The people who made profits that were the envy of corporations in Europe and North America did not own the land on which they constructed their trading empires. The windfall gains were captured by the colonial government through regular auctions. One benefit was the low tax regime, which enabled investors to maximise profits from their capital. This philosophy permeates private enterprise to this day.

The MTR Corporation was established in Hong Kong in 1975 to construct and operate a mass transit railway on prudent commercial principles (see Box 4). It operates six railway lines totalling 88 kilometres and 49 stations. Its Property Director, Thomas Ho, stresses the intimate relationship between those who travel on their trains and the lifestyles they enjoy: 'One of the most attractive elements of our properties is their location. People enjoy working, living and shopping in properties located directly above or adjacent to railway stations, as they offer convenience, added value and efficiency.'[2]

Who pays for this integrated transport and urban lifestyle? Not the taxpayers of Hong Kong. In fact, the government expects a net gain out of the arrangement. It supplies the land at the market price. MTR Corporation operates as the intermediate agency linking property companies to the people who would buy or rent the apartments and shops. According to Ho:

> From the government's perspective, there is no cost associated with the granting of development rights to the Corporation. They obtain the full market value of the land (referred to as 'land premium') for each site from us and in turn, we tender the sites out and award them to the successful developers. Our profits are derived, not from the government, but from developers who offer a share of profits to us.[3]

In 2002, the corporation achieved a net profit of HK$4.2 billion (US$540 million), with profit from property at HK$3.7 billion (US$481 million) and property rental and management

---

2   Interview under the title 'Property as a means of financing railway infrastructure', *Public Transport International*, 6, 2003, p. 33.

3   Ibid., p. 32.

Box 4 **The philosophy of property**

In its *Facts and Information* publication, MTR Corporation spells out its philosophy on property: 'Railways, particularly urban underground systems, are recognised to stimulate property development opportunities and enhance land values along their route networks.'

Bottom-line profits are maximised when entrepreneurs – even those whose majority shareholder happens to be the government – view their investments in holistic terms. 'As communities that are comprehensively developed in conjunction with the railway stations [they] will be positioned to form some of the most desirable business, residential and shopping centres with a certain degree of self-sufficiency in terms of social and recreational amenities, retailing provisions and employment opportunities.'

MTR chiefs have their feet firmly planted on the ground, but their aspirations are sky high. 'The Corporation obtains government consent to develop air space above or adjacent to the railway sites.' Deals are done with property developers to build at their cost, to the corporation's standards. 'These costs include the payment of government land premium, construction, finance and other professional costs. The Corporation derives benefit when the property is sold, through the sharing of profits with the developers.'

Community amenities add to asset values. Developments 'include areas of open space, recreational facilities, community and infrastructural provisions to ensure that each development produces a fully integrated and quality environment'.

income at HK$987 million (US$126 million). Thus, a transport agency is able to work with the land market to yield a net gain for itself and for the citizens of Hong Kong. Investors in the property companies receive their dividends from the profits of constructing the new urban experience. This model confounds the cherished beliefs hoarded by Western transport planners over the past 40 years.

The MTRC was charged with exploiting its property assets, the value of which soon became more valuable than the Railway Corporation itself!

Between 1972 and 1985, MTRC undertook projects that included two cross-harbour tunnels, a new airport and additional railways. In January 2000 its 50-year exclusive franchise to operate Hong Kong's rail started. Although the government was a 77 per cent owner, the corporation was required to operate like a private company. It is one of the largest estate managers in Hong Kong, with 36,700 residential units as well as office and retail space. It embarked on joint venture developments on the Kowloon and Airport Express stations. The Kowloon project includes a 102-storey landmark tower. On the Airport Express, property developments resulted in HK$3.3 billion profits. It has been in profit for the last ten years. Rail operations delivered a net profit. For the first six months of 2005, MTR's interim net profit (including a gain on property revaluations of HK$1.02 billion) was HK$2.61 billion (Lau, 2005). The travelling public benefits from this remarkable performance: the fares they pay have been frozen since 1997.

In the MTR Annual Report 2000, the chairman's statement discussed the unique business model, deriving significant benefits from integrating our railway business with the development of substantial properties in conjunction with our railway stations and depots. Providing an efficient transport service has enhanced the attractiveness of properties situated at MTR stations. On the other hand, building communities along MTR lines has enhanced patronage and supplemented the return on our railway investments. Building on the foundations of our successful railway, property and other commercial businesses, we have gained access to a substantial proportion of Hong Kong's population, comprising an average of approximately 2.3m passenger trips per weekday on the railway, approximately 170,000 residents living and working in properties managed by the MTR, [with] approximately 160,000 visitors per day to our shopping centres.

This property philosophy did not obscure the need to expand the rail network 'on the basis of a commercial rate of return'. Even so, noted the chairman, 'new railway lines will also open up further opportunities for property development and commercial activities. Competition from other transport modes had contributed to a drop in patronage in the first half of 2000, which spurred the corporation to control costs and improve efficiency'.

MTR vigorously promotes public awareness of its activities, which include seven developments costing HK$50 billion (£4.6 billion).

- 16 residential towers containing 5,600 units;
- a 102-storey landmark tower comprising offices of 231,778 square metres, a deluxe hotel of 330 rooms and an observation deck;

- a 64-storey block accommodating 1,100 service apartments and 220 residential units;
- a 64-storey high-quality hotel block;
- a world-class shopping centre of 82,750 square metres;
- transport interchange for public buses, cross-border coaches, minibuses, taxis, hotel shuttle and tour buses;
- more than 6,000 car parking spaces.

Five property development complexes are being built along the Airport Express, totalling 3.3 million square metres. 'The planning and design of these complexes focus on creating communities that are fully integrated with the railway stations. Some 27,000 flats and 1.3m sq. m. of commercial space will be generated from these station developments' (MTR Corporation, n.d.: 1).

The corporation appears to deliver satisfaction to its 470,000 retail shareholders, as well as its major institutional investors. As for the government, its role as the owner of land in Hong Kong has not confused the approach to property markets or the needs of entrepreneurship. The more prosperous the economy, the more people are willing to pay for the right to exclusive leasehold possession of sites!

Hong Kong's need for an expanded transit system is emphasised by demographic realities. A population of 6.9 million is predicted to grow to 8 million by 2016. With the completion of twelve new railway projects by 2016, the network will have expanded from 143 kilometres to over 250 kilometres. About 70 per cent of the total population and 80 per cent of employment will then be within walking distance of railway stations. The pressing need to transfer people from cars to trains can be detected from the data in Table 4.

In its post-colonial phase, Hong Kong has to service a rapidly expanding flow of capital into its economic hinterland. The Kowloon and Canton Railway Corporation (KCRC) operates the rail link between Kowloon and the border and the light rail system in the North West New Territories. It is owned by the government, but it is also required to operate on commercial principles. It has made a profit for more than ten years. The profit in 2000 was HK$2.3 billion. This corporation is engaged in massive infrastructure and property-related developments to expand the commercial ties with mainland China.

KCRC also develops commercial properties above or near its stations. Like the MTR, it has not raised fares since 1997. Some of its services lose money, with profitability sustained by the cross-border market and property interests. Government does not take a dividend. It allows KCRC to accumulate profits – to retain enhanced land values to fund new rail projects.

In terms of Hypothesis I, *it is not tenable to argue that railways must necessarily rely on subsidies from taxpayers*.[4]

Singapore: bidding for space

When space is scarce, people are willing to pay a rent for the privilege of monopolising it. In Singapore, market mechanisms have been developed that equalise everyone's ability to share in the benefits of that scarcity. Motorists are free to determine the road rents they are willing to pay. They do so at auctions where they

4 During the colonial era, public investment in infrastructure in Hong Kong automatically yielded higher returns than an equivalent project funded in Britain. That was because the colonial government in Hong Kong funded its projects out of the rent of land, so there was no deadweight-loss hurdle to overcome of the kind that confronted similar projects in Britain.

Table 4 **Road Realities (1998)**

	Km per 1,000 people	Motor vehicles per km road	Motor vehicles per 1,000 people
Hong Kong	0.28	268.5	75
Singapore	0.99	218.3	215
UK	6.69	71.3	477
USA	23.30	33.6	783

Source: *Transtat*, Hong Kong: Transport Bureau, October 2001

compete to secure the right to drive on the highways. Those who fail in their bids, or who have no wish to own a car, share in the benefits of the road rents which are spent on providing first-class public transport.

The imperative need for rationing is stressed by the data in Table 4. Singapore is an overcrowded island where, if a curb were not placed on the growth of vehicles, life would be intolerable. The government has constrained the growth of vehicles to 3 per cent a year. A range of tools are used, including the Certificate of Entitlement (COE), the Vehicle Quota System (VQS), road taxes and Electronic Road Pricing (ERP).

Each month, a certain number of COEs are released. The vehicle entitlement is valid for ten years from the date of registration of the vehicle. Bidding is by electronic means by which people determine how much they will pay in competition with other would-be motorists.

Electronic road pricing is based on the pay-per-use principle that reflects the true cost of motoring. It has been extended to points of congestion on major highways and is credited with having reduced the volume of traffic during peak periods.

The outcome is a cost of motoring that appears horrendous. Some estimates (in Singapore dollars) are: for an Audi A41.8:

$182,000; for a BMW 328 (2.8 cc): $238,000; for a Mercedes 200E: $201,902; for a Volvo 940 Turbo Estate 2.0: $160,753. The alternative is to go by bus or train! That demand for COEs almost always exceeds supply is confirmed by the consistent rise in prices. Auctions are open, meaning that bidders are able to observe others' bids before they submit their offers. This avoids the risk of people recklessly overbidding.

The World Bank has concluded that Singapore's transport policies have helped to attract foreign investment, and that there are no major negative side effects on economic growth or on the welfare of people on the lowest incomes. In addition, 'rationing scarce physical space by the price mechanism ... generated large funds for investment in improvements much beyond transport, and enabled reductions of other, less desirable taxes' (Willoughby, 2000: iii).

This is a truly integrated transport policy. Those who cannot afford to run a car benefit from higher-quality public transport and lower taxes. That is a compensation deal that turns everyone into a winner. Road rents facilitate a sophisticated approach to sharing scarce space. The collateral gains include a dynamic economy at the frontier of technological progress, and wage levels that are the envy of employees in the rich nations of the West.

Commentators generally fail to link the road rents regime with Singapore's low tax rates. But the government is conscious that success in the global markets depends on their being able to recycle rents back into the island's infrastructure so that equity is associated with efficiency. Large fortunes are made in Singapore, but these tend to be earned rather than the result of windfalls. The housing sector illustrates the point. The government, in providing highways, does not expect to reward landowners while penalising taxpayers (which is the UK political model). So when land is compulsorily purchased to provide public housing, it has to be sold to the state at agricultural-use prices. Far from undermining the free market, this policy is used to bolster an enterprising economy which places Singapore at the forefront of global commerce.

Today, 86 per cent of Singaporeans live in public housing towns. Their arteries are the road and rail networks which, if allowed to become sclerotic in the way familiar to Europeans and North Americans, would quickly cause seizure in Singapore. About 63 per cent of motorised trips are by public transport. The Singapore philosophy is that travel is always for a purpose, and that it therefore makes sense to integrate land use and transport by locating homes, offices and recreational amenities in appropriate proximity to transport amenities. Singapore's free market ethic is not affronted by her stress on the need for planning, because the two are viewed as working in tandem to produce the best possible outcomes for everyone with a stake in the city-state.

In terms of Hypothesis II, *it is not tenable to believe that road pricing is financially or technologically unrealistic, or that it disadvantages people on the lowest incomes.*

Japan: shopping for efficiency

Britain played a significant role in the construction of railways in Japan. The first line was built in 1872, between Tokyo and Shimbashi. By 1945, more than 25,600 kilometres of lines existed. National Railways operated 20,056 kilometres of lines, private railways operated 5,543 kilometres. By 1981, the JNR (Japanese National Railways) system was 21,418 kilometres long.

But while the technology may have been imported, the funding arrangements were inspired by the emperor in the 1870s (Harrison, 1983: ch. 11). Rising farmland rents were invested in the infrastructure that delivered what was to become the second-wealthiest nation in the world. Japan's entrepreneurs also understood the intimate relationship between capital investment in railways and the rents that were externalised through the land market. That emerges as a historical lesson of major significance. A second lesson, from the privatisation programme of 1987, is that market principles were necessary to achieve maximum efficiency in the use of labour.

The novel feature of Japan's railways originated at the beginning of the twentieth century. Entrepreneurs developed their commercial interests by associating department stores with the construction of their own railways. The tracks were run from the suburbs and the terminus was at the store itself. The railway brought in the customers. The externalised value of the investment in the railway was internalised into the profits of the store, which funded the capital costs of the tracks.

Railways generated added value at both ends of the track. At the residential end, land values rose beneath the homes of families living in the suburbs. At the commercial end, land values rose beneath the retail properties. The capture of the additional value beneath commercial buildings was sufficient to enable the railways to operate profitably. They did not need subsidies from taxpayers. This mechanism was used to regenerate communities after the devastation of World War II. Rents were the catalyst for the emergence of diversified enterprises. During the 1950s and 1960s many private rail companies built lines that 'frequently served as anchors for real estate and commercial development projects. Private rail companies subsequently diversified their commercial interests outside the transport sector into activities such as hotel and retail operations, as their real estate projects developed' (Kopicki et al., 1995: 75).[5]

Private rail networks provided the major component of Japan's urban and commuter services. One of these was the Odakyu Electric Railway Company Ltd. It was established in 1948, but its origins go back to the Odawara Express Railway Company Ltd (founded in 1923). Its small network of 120 kilometres of tracks served commuters between residential suburbs and Tokyo city centre. Originally, it was built to serve shopping centres. The company continues to operate department stores, tourist facilities that include hotels, and other real estate interests. Then, as the world embarked on the Information Age, it demonstrated its capacity to move with the times. Odakyu realised that it could extract additional rents from its tracks by laying fibre-optic cables. From April 2001 it leased these to two Internet service providers and cable TV companies. With daily passengers totalling 1.8 million, it is investing in new tracks to reduce travel times. Funds are from banks and shareholders. Despite its debt, it remains profitable and pays a 10 per cent dividend to shareholders.

The disasters of World War II required a regeneration programme, and the Japanese government decided to develop a national strategy that would integrate the networks. The JNR was established as a public corporation in 1949. It proved by its size to be too awkward to respond to the needs of passengers and shippers. It found competition from private railways awkward to handle, its operations were hampered by government

---

5   This account of the Japanese story draws heavily on Chapter 5 of Kopicki et al. (1995).

intervention, inadequate management incentives and labour unions that were protected from market competition.

Technologically, Japan was at the forefront. The first high-speed Shinkansen (bullet train) was introduced in the 1960s. Technology was not matched by the financial performance of the JNR. Its crisis began in the late 1950s. Its market share was eroded by private railway companies. The first operating loss surfaced in 1964. By 1985 it was generating losses at an annual rate of $20 billion. In 1987, when it was privatised, it could not deliver enough money to service its debt. The government's annual $5 billion subsidy was insufficient.

Unlike its private competitors, the nationalised network was profligate in the use of labour. The JNR hoarded people. At one point, labour costs were 78 per cent of total revenues on the JNR compared with 40 per cent for private railways. Observing a general shift away from rail traffic, 'private railways responded with profit-oriented operational strategies to cope with the changed competitive environment. In contrast, JNR continues to expand its unprofitable remote railway network, on the grounds that it was a public service-oriented enterprise. Remote railway routes accounted for more than 40 per cent of the lines run by JNR but represented only 5 per cent of total transport volume', observed the World Bank (ibid.: 83).

Were these 'remote' routes really drains on the JNR's profit-and-loss account? How did the World Bank know? In the private sector, rail-related land values were monitored through the assets of railway/real estate enterprises. In the public sector, the national accounts failed to offer a comprehensive audit that included the rents that could be attributed to the railways. The strikingly large JNR debt does not help us to reach a conclusion. The allegedly unprofitable railways of Europe reported 'deficits' that were addressed through subsidies, so no debt was carried over to the following financial year. JNR's debt ballooned because its annual deficits were covered by borrowing money. It first borrowed to cover an operational cost shortfall in 1971. By 1987, the debt was US\$337 billion. Ideally, we would like to compare that debt with the value of land of remotely located owners whose assets generated rents because of the punctual arrival and departure of the JNR trains.

The JNR debt was assigned to the Japan National Railways Settlement Corporation in 1987, along with surplus real estate and shares in the newly created Japanese Railways (JRs). It was out of these assets that the JNR Settlement Corporation endowed a fund with income-generating securities to cover the revenue shortfall and capital costs of the three island JRs.

A measure of the constraints on enterprise driven by the public sector's influence is suggested by what happened after privatisation. Employment was reduced in the JRs from 200,650 (1986) to 132,296 employees (1991). But the JNR had not only hoarded labour. Under privatisation, a large amount of undeveloped land was sold, including 3,917 hectares in 1992. The railways had contributed to the land speculation boom of the late 1980s.

Once privatised, the financial fortunes of the individual companies were transformed. This was reflected in the public finances: *the annual \$5 billion drain on the Treasury was turned into a net cash flow contribution of \$3.1 billion in 1991.*

Today, Japan has 148 rail companies, grouped into four types.

1   The JR Group. This is the former JNR. It is the single national mainline and freight company that was split in

1987 into six regional and one freight-operating private companies.

2   The urban private rail companies. These operate largely as commuter services. The majority are associated with department store and real estate companies. They own the infrastructure. Some facilities are shared between several train networks.

3   The publicly owned underground. Some local authorities operate subway systems. The Tokyo subway has twelve lines.

4   Small rural operations. These include many reportedly non-profitable local services which are operated by 'third sector' agencies involving local governments or prefectures.[6]

Since 1987, the government's role has been limited to maintaining the national infrastructure on the advice of the Transport Policy Council. The government assumes all or some of the investment cost and the risk in relation to infrastructure on the grounds of national development, and allegedly because this is beyond the capacity of private companies. This belief is undermined by the performance of the private railway/real estate companies. Odakyu's track-widening programme in 2002 was privately funded.

Because of the deeper relationship between operating costs and land values, the three largest JR companies and most of the urban companies such as Odakyu are profitable. While these companies are frequently associated with other commercial operations, the transport businesses are profitable, and are deemed not to be dependent on subsidies from, for example, their association with department stores.

6   We have no estimates of the potential decline (if any) in land values if those local services were withdrawn.

The privatised rail companies are vertically integrated. They control tracks, signalling and rolling stock up to the commercial activities associated with real estate at the stations. Japanese managements believe that ownership of, or responsibility for, the infrastructure provides them with the incentive to invest capital. They believe in first-rate tracks being necessary for first-rate rolling stock. In contrast to the British system of limited-life franchises, there are no such curbs on Japan's companies. They own the infrastructure for as long as they remain in business; similarly where the infrastructure is leased.

JR East is the largest railway company on the eastern end of Honshu. It has 7,538 kilometres of tracks and carries 16 million passengers every day. Its profits come from merchandise sales, shopping centres and hotels. Operating revenues have reached $20.1 billion. Fares are set on the basis of marginal costs. They have remained unchanged since 1987, which means they are considerably lower than UK rail fares. Infrastructural investment is funded out of the land values that are recycled back into the operation through the real estate interests.

Some rail companies do make 'losses'. Osaka's Nankai Railway Company undertook staff reductions in 2002 to deal with its deficit. Three companies that operate on the islands would not be financially viable without funding from the Railway Management Stabilisation Fund. This is composed of the rail assets that were retained by government. Income from the fund is allocated to invest in infrastructure on the islands. Funds are also allocated where a 'social' need is perceived. For example, some JR companies were reluctant to abandon some of the social obligations that were acknowledged by the publicly owned rail organisation, and they are unwilling to close loss-making local lines. A full accounting would reveal whether land values in those localities would decline if the rail services were withdrawn.

While the financial performance of the private railway companies speaks for itself, Japan lost its fiscal way in the twentieth century. The emperor's optimum pricing policies became a victim of the democratisation of the political process. But the Japanese government continues to search for ways to align transport with its scarce landed assets. In January 2001 the ministries of construction and transport were merged into the Ministry of Land Infrastructure and Transport (MLIT). Its mission is to integrate land use and transport 'through the comprehensive and systematic utilisation, development and conservation of land, integrated improvement of infrastructure and the pursuit of innovative transport policy'.

The economic realities of mass transit systems have been corrupted by policy errors, so that even the most seasoned transport chiefs, such as Bob Kiley, whose success in operating New York's metro led to his appointment as London's Traffic Commissioner, could erroneously claim: 'There is not a transport system in the world which is run without public subsidy. There is no break-even transit system anywhere.'[7]

Our review of the evidence from the Far East casts a completely new light on transport economics. In terms of Hypothesis III, *the notion that the only model for railways is state ownership based on the power of the public purse is discredited.*

The general conclusion is unambiguous. The way in which a community uses and distributes the rent of land is the key to achieving optimum efficiency and the solution to problems that

---

7   Bob Kiley, interview on *The Politics Programme*, BBC1, 19 October 2003.

have hitherto defeated governments. We need a deeper assessment of rent and the role of the state. People need to know that
there are penalties for not paying the market price for the use of
highways, for example, as happens in Singapore. Under-payment
has a reciprocal effect in the land market. One illustration is what
happened to the value of the UK's housing stock over the ten years
to 2004: it increased by 200 per cent, reaching £3.3 trillion (50 per
cent higher than in 2001, according to Halifax). If motorists had
to pay the market price for using the highways, they would end up
bidding less for residential property. As it was, under-payment for
the use of roads contributed to the house price barrier that denied
affordable homes to many people.

5   THE RENT-OPTIMISING GOAL

The dynamics of location

Inefficient ways of funding transport reduce the productivity of firms and discredit governments. A comprehensive framework is needed within which to locate the damaging spillover effects. The classical economists provided a model of the system at work that became the core of the science of political economy.

Adam Smith (1776 [1981]) provided the template for analysing the emerging industrial mode of production. He disaggregated the producers of wealth into three factors: land, labour and capital. Their shares of the nation's income were classified as rent, wages and interest. Land was plausibly treated as a contributor to wealth because nature's fertility played a role in the output of employees and capital. In that sense, land 'earned' the rent that was attributed to it. The variations in rental payments by tenant farmers were said to be due to variations in the fertility of the soil. A natural law was at work, based on the reproductive capacity of land. This did not mean that the people who possessed the title deeds to land had *earned* the rent. In any event, this portrait of the natural economy provided a satisfactory model for analysing the production and distribution of income that existed in the second half of the eighteenth century.

A more complex analytical framework was needed for manufacturing. The three-factor model was insufficiently elaborate to highlight important features associated with the concentration of people and capital in confined locations.

Land was of diminishing relevance in terms of its fertility. Now, *location* emerged as paramount. Nature played a lesser role except in so far as she freely provided the land and natural resources that were needed.[1] No longer could rent be configured almost exclusively in terms of fertility. A new way of characterising these payments was required.

Today the claimants of rent base their demands not on the argument that they create wealth, because – qua landowners – they do not do so. Their claim rests exclusively on ownership of title deeds. The law sanctions the payment often on the basis of the outcome of the struggle for power in the age of feudalism.[2] In the meantime, however, the significance of land in particular locations changed rapidly in response to the new demands people made on their communities. Government, as well as enforcing law and order and defending the realm, assumed responsibility for public health. With so many people migrating out of the countryside and coalescing around factories and mines, it was necessary to invest capital in new systems for the delivery of water, energy and waste disposal. Those resources had to come from somewhere.

After Adam Smith, David Ricardo (1772–1823) explained why funding could come from one source only: the rent of land. *Rent*

---

1   Agricultural land did continue to operate as a device for transferring income. Among all OECD countries, the subsidies to agriculture in 2004 totalled nearly $380 billion. The European Union privileged its food producers with $133 billion, which was more than 40 per cent of the EU budget (Williams, 2005).

2   Lawyers correlate rent to shares in the 'bundle of rights' associated with land. It is these rights which are owned, not the land itself.

was the measure of the taxable capacity of the economy. A switch-back mechanism was needed in the financial architecture. The smooth distribution of income to fund intensive investment in the community's infrastructure was vital if Britain were to enjoy to the full the new age of abundance.

It was necessary to redefine land. We may use the concept of *location* to represent the way in which people choose to share services in common. These services, when combined with labour and capital, improve the productivity of the economy and the quality of people's lives (which, of course, enhances their productive capacities). Location was the point at which people were able to express the sum of the value of the services that met their needs. The public space became operationally central to the market economy's ability to realise the potential that was made possible by scientific and technological progress and the commercial scale on which people operated.

Income is still divided between wages, interest and rent (Figure 1). Rent is retained because it represents the value commanded by each site. But the financial needs of the new economy meant that rent ought to have been subdivided into two categories.

- Part of rental revenue needed to be switched back into infrastructure. This is the price people were willing to pay for the benefits received at the locations they occupied.
- The remainder of rent could be devoted to non-subsistence consumption. In the historical conditions prevailing in the late eighteenth century, it was not politically practical to capture the whole of rent to pay for public services (to do so would have entailed the abnegation of the landowners who dominated Parliament). So part of it would flow to the

Figure 1   **The social model of production**

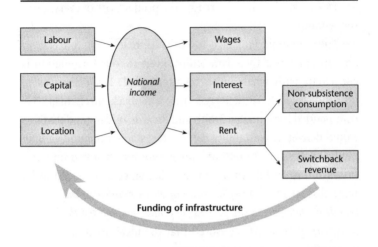

owners of land as a transfer payment. As such, it would fund their private conspicuous consumption.

Thus, there was the price of labour (wages), the price of capital (interest) and the aggregate rental price of the cumulative benefits that were accessed in particular locations.

Rent is the surplus net of taxes which is capitalised into the selling price of land. It is symmetrical to the value of the benefits that people receive. These benefits are complex, but the market enables people to put a price on them. Rent reflects the exhaustible resources provided by nature (topsoil, fish, minerals), inexhaustible resources provided by nature (location, the frequency spectrum), value generated by infrastructure (such as railways) and the value generated by private activity (for example, the ingenuity of George Stephenson, who invented the steam engine for use on wheels, which increased the productivity of everyone in the economy).

The economic language for this approach was not elaborated in our terms by Adam Smith. Even so, our formulation is consistent with what Smith recommended. His principles of taxation *would* have delivered the switchback mechanism. He commended the land tax. Smith and Ricardo understood that this would deliver price stability. Unlike taxes on labour and capital, public charges on the rent of land are not incorporated into unit prices and passed down the chain to fall on consumers (Ricardo, 1817: chs. 10 and 12). *So the price of goods retailed in the markets reflects the labour and capital costs of production, but not the location attributes of land.*[3] This ensured that the ideal fiscal system was consistent with the market economy.

Understanding the role of rent and location was central to progress. The theory of rent was deepened by Ricardo in terms which, had it influenced public policy, would have enabled the capitalist economy to function more efficiently. The key was the recommendation of a modernised land tax. Parliament did not act on this advice.

Ricardo's work has been criticised for employing an agricultural model. In fact, while he did emphasise the 'original and indestructible powers' of land, in Chapter 2 of *On the Principles of Political Economy and Taxation* (1817) he also alerted readers to a further distinguishing characteristic. Some sites 'possessed

---

3   Ricardo (1817: ch. 11) was emphatic about the significance of the discovery that 'rent does not and cannot enter in the least degree' in prices. In a footnote, he stated: 'Clearly understanding this principle is, I am persuaded, of the utmost importance to the science of political economy' (p. 40).

peculiar advantages of situation', while others were 'less advantageously situated'. Location was made explicit as a variable, one that would assume increasing importance as people and capital accumulated in the great centres of manufacturing and trade such as Birmingham, Manchester and Glasgow.[4]

Smith and Ricardo identified a conduit for recycling value back into funding the nation's shared services. Part of that value was the result of infrastructure. This became a new claim on rents. The land market afforded the mechanism for concentrating, measuring and reallocating the rents. The institutional framework was in place to serve the economy. But in accounting terms, too many books were not being balanced. The partnership that ought to have emerged to synchronise the public and private sectors did not come into play. Are we living with the consequences? Can the great economic dislocations of the nineteenth century be traced to the failure to connect the junction boxes linking the nation's income to the factors that produced it? One thing is certain. Now, in the 21st century, policy-makers are struggling to develop hybrid models of the market–state partnership. This is illustrated in the transport sector. Can the hybrids neutralise the leakages and losses of the past? Or are they also doomed to failure?

'A peculiar tax'

Capitalism triumphed over communism in the 1980s, but within a decade the philosophy of market economics was once again challenged, this time from within. People who did not associate

---

4   Ricardo (1817) discusses Smith's treatment of location in *Principles*, ch. 24 (p. 198).

themselves with socialist doctrines held the market responsible for social and ecological problems. To test the validity of this censure of market economics we must return to Adam Smith.

Smith knew that if the division of labour was to work to everyone's advantage the appropriate institutions had to be constructed. The genius and commitment of the individual would have to be partnered with corresponding laws and social processes. His vision of the inclusive community embraced everyone who wanted to earn a living. Poverty would not be institutionalised. Smith elaborated a theory of a moral society that integrated politics and ethics with economics. He elegantly synthesised competition and cooperation so that everyone who contributed to the wealth of the nation was a beneficiary:

- *Competition* ensures the swiftest route to optimum efficiency. Unit costs of labour and capital are equalised as scientific and technological progress increases people's productive capacity.
- *Cooperation* ensures that the net benefits of the competitive spirit are equalised across the population. Increasing productivity reduces the inputs needed to generate incomes, delivering rents that could be used to pay for shared services.

The benefits people receive from the community have been called the 'social wage'. Thus, we see the genius of Smith's model. The specialisation of labour does not lead to the division of the community. Increasing prosperity would be grounded in the unity of cooperation and competition; these were made to intersect harmoniously by synchronising the public and private sectors. This outcome was contingent on funding shared services out of rents. Since rents (generally speaking) were not earned by any one person, everyone would enjoy the gain through the expenditure of rents from the community chest.[5]

The labour theory of value was morally significant in Smith's vision. Value was thought to be contingent on the expenditure of labour; labour thought to be the moral basis of rights to the product of one's work. From this, it followed that claims to a share of the wealth to which one has not contributed are ill founded. A person cannot be – or rather, *ought not to be* – separated from the value that he or she creates. Exchange is based on like-for-like value, as perceived by those engaged in the negotiation. Thus, while wages and the returns on one's savings remain in private hands, rents were the legitimate source of public revenue.

Smith's principle on rents as public revenue was not an optional extra to be bolted on to the market economy. Enterprise – through competition – systematically generates the conditions in which part of the wealth of the nation is forced out of the labour and capital markets. That value then cascades down to be collected as rent, distributing itself in proportion to the variable qualities of location, soil and other natural and social attributes. Through the national exchequer, that rent may be reintegrated into the community for the benefit of everyone. Smith was emphatic: rents were 'peculiarly suitable' for defraying the expenses of the state: 'Ground-rents, and the ordinary rent of land, are, there-fore, perhaps, the species of revenue which can best bear to have a peculiar tax imposed upon them' (Smith, 1776 [1981]: 844).

The community and the economy that he visualised would

---

5 We acknowledge the role of the individual in the production of rental income, as in the seminal case of George Stephenson's impact on land values in the north-east of England. Did he and his shareholders, those who invested their savings in his railway, have a direct claim on rent? See Chapter 6.

Box 5 **The sin of omission**

Markets are the sum total of individual interactions that lead to the production, distribution and exchange of wealth. The processes that facilitate this economic behaviour are based on two sets of rules. The first flows from the nature of humans (such as the propensity to satisfy our needs with the least possible exertion). The other is composed of the laws and institutions that facilitate human propensities. If there are impediments to the efficiency of markets, these tend to be in the laws that frame the markets.

The doctrine of market failure needs to be challenged for reasons beyond semantics. Economists colour people's political views by appearing to attribute serious and protracted problems – such as poverty – to market failures. In fact, poverty is offensive to the market system, which requires 'effective demand' to make the exchange of goods and services possible. The larger the demand, the more efficient the economy and the greater the rental surplus.

The land market is cited as a classic case of so-called market failure: 'Land use decisions are superimposed on a settlement pattern based on massive market failure in land. The phenomena rather imprecisely called "land speculation" and "absentee ownership" betray market failure; and no one disputes there is massive regulatory failure in pricing and subsidising transportation, which in turn determine land rents and values. Result: the land market is not efficient; land is not properly priced and allocated to begin with.'

But this inefficiency does not stem from the intrinsic logic of markets per se. The description is by Mason Gaffney (1988: 133–54), who acknowledges that the failure is linked to 'public programmes and perverse incentives ... [and] the quest for unearned increments to land value'. Unearned increments offend the principle of exchanging value added to the economy through enterprise. Correctly analysed, failures are the result of sins of omission by government.

need government, which had to draw its resources from some-where, but which should not do so in a manner that interfered with people who work, save and invest.

A public charge on the rent of land was an ancient doctrine that happened to fulfil the norms of efficiency in a market economy. And so, in an age of radical intellectual accomplish-ments – in which scientists and engineers were transforming abstract ideas into practical solutions for the creation of wealth at a wondrous rate – Smith held firm on the need to be conservative in his doctrine of governance: 'Nothing can be more reasonable than that a fund which owes its existence to the good govern-ment of the state, should be taxed peculiarly, or should contribute something more than the greater part of other funds, towards the support of that government' (ibid.: 844).

The recommendation was not adopted. This led to economic crises that are now rationalised by the doctrine of 'market failure' (see Box 5). The outcome was the resort to non-market solutions to fund the infrastructure that made the state viable. Does the state now need to rescue itself by belatedly resurrecting Smith's model of governance?

All roads lead to Rome

Ours may be the age of virtual reality, but conventional modes of transport will continue to be vital to the future of the state. But the best-laid plans are worthless if the resources are not avail-able to fund them. A curious feature of the transport industry is its pessimism about being able to pay for roads and railways. The House of Commons Transport Select Committee (2003: 56) framed this message of despair in these terms:

> However, even if all the local transport schemes offered
> value for money they could not be afforded … It is
> inevitable therefore that fewer public transport schemes
> than proposed will be implemented. This means more
> journeys will be made by car and congestion will rise,
> particularly in the city areas where these schemes would be
> most effective.

If transport schemes are of the value-for-money kind, why is it not possible to harness that value to pay for the schemes? The MPs did not address this question, but this was not exceptional. The Department for Transport is similarly afflicted by the despair. It paid consultants to elaborate schemes which could 'not be afforded within the 10 Year Plan budget, despite this being the intention of the Plan' (ibid.: 56).

It is difficult to believe that the apparent ineptitude displayed in the transport sector can be attributed purely to administrative incompetence.[6] Persistent failures suggest the probability of a flaw in the philosophy of transportation.

State planning has detached transport from its spatial and financial underpinnings. In a complex commercial society, transport needs to be integrated into its web of interrelationships, the ordering of which requires a sophisticated and flexible decision-making process. Planning methodology necessarily retreats to simplifications that do not adequately reflect economic realities,

---

6 Incompetence may be attributed to individual projects. This would appear to explain the expensive failure of Britain's west coast mainline upgrade, which was supposed to cost £3 billion but would cost £10 billion by the time the work was completed – and even then, the track would not be able to take the high-speed trains for which it was supposed to be constructed. What he calls the incompetence, greed and delusion behind Britain's biggest single infrastructure project was documented by Meek (2004).

and political decisions cannot keep pace with people's changing aspirations. The ligaments of the sophisticated system are to be discerned in the transport philosophy of the Roman Empire.

If the Romans did not have a coherent philosophy of transport, they successfully acted as if they did. We know that, logistically, they could build fine highways, but this was just one element of a triadic system of circulation that advanced the imperial project.

Highways had to serve a *military* purpose. The physical structure and spatial orientation of the roads had to fulfil two purposes:

- *Minimum mobility costs*: the rapid movement of soldiers around the territory at the least possible expenditure of human energy.
- *Maximum defensive postures*: an army marching through exposed terrain is vulnerable to bends (around which nasty surprises might lurk). Elevation prevents hostile forces from looking down on the legions. Roads, consequently, were straight, and configured to hug the high ground.

Highways also had to circulate *information*. The postal network was crucial if the political centre was to retain direct control over extensive territories. The average distance achieved by the postal service was 50 miles per day.

Highways, however, could not be treated as separate from the *financial* system. How were the roads to be funded? Their solution: *out of locally derived rents*. This ensured that each section of the highway was self-funding, and therefore not a burden on the imperial centre. The roads were designed to provide a measure of distance, and to serve the mutual interests of farmers and the state. Improved access to markets increased productivity. Farmers also benefited by 'letting some parts of the estate out to tenant farmers and pocketing the rents' (Wilkinson, 2001: 52). Roads were also used to provide the measure of land that 'could be beneficial when it came to levying taxes, which were often based on the area of land held by the locals' (ibid.: 92). This was the world's first integrated transport system. The level of integration provided access to markets in regions that would otherwise be inaccessible, and was financed in a way that would not be a fiscal burden on the Roman economy.

By acting locally, Rome found a way to construct a global transport network that is admired to this day. The highways stretched all the way from Hadrian's Wall in the north of England through continental Europe to Rome itself. And we, it appears, after 60 years of fruitless searching, are not able to find a solution to funding Crossrail to bisect 20 miles of London.

Markets as society's mediator

Transport planners confess that they lack a theory that integrates transport with the economy. This void achieves embarrassing proportions with confessions in their literature. Adam Smith, on the other hand, did elaborate the elements of a coherent philosophy of transport. These appear in the lectures on jurisprudence he delivered at Glasgow University. If his economy was constructed on the division of labour, the foundations were cemented into the theory of rent and public finance.

Gains from the production of wealth were contingent on the size of the market, which determines the degree to which people could refine their skills. The division of labour 'must always be proportioned to the extent of commerce. If 10 people only want a certain commodity, the manufacture of it will never be so divided as if a thousand wanted it'. The size of the market, in turn, was contingent on transport. Smith (1766 [1982]: 494) noted in a lecture:

> Again, the division of labour, in order to opulence, becomes always more perfect by the easy method of conveyance in a country. If the road be infested with robbers, if it be deep and conveyance not easy, the progress of commerce must be stopped. Since the mending of roads in England 40 or 50 years ago, its opulence has increased extremely.

Moral sentiments were not in conflict with economic efficiency. It was, Smith specified, essential that the price of labour should be sufficient to enable people to participate in production. Wages had to provide people with sufficient subsistence to maintain themselves and their families, and to cover the costs of education and health (ibid.: 575). Smith did not see any contradiction in fusing normative with positive statements – if the purpose of economics as a science was optimal outcomes. Commerce *could* operate efficiently to enable people to meet their material needs in a way (for example) that would obviate demands for a welfare state. But, he noted in an early draft of *The Wealth of Nations*, the market price for labour was contingent on there not being 'some great error in the public polic[y]'. Taxes levied on industry were a policy error. They obstructed 'a natural balance of industry [which] tends to break this balance [and] tends to hurt national or public opulence' (ibid.: 575). Bounties levied on the manufacture or export of goods had this effect. The way in which taxes damage productivity and therefore the circulation of goods was illustrated by reference to the era of horse-and-carts, but the causal connections remain valid for the age of jet travel:

> Of the bounty upon corn. That it has sunk the price of corn, and thereby tends to lower the rents of corn farms. That by diminishing the number [of grass farms], it tends to raise the rent of grass farms, to raise the price of butcher meat, the price of hay, the expense of keeping horses, and consequently the price of carriage, which must, so far, embarrass the whole inland commerce of the country. (Ibid.: 575)

Smith's model is completed by his treatment of the way in which the state raises its revenue. Public charges on rent do not raise prices or distort investment and production:

> Ground-rents are a still more proper subject of taxation than the rent of houses. A tax upon it would fall altogether upon the owner of the ground-rent, who acts always as a monopolist, and exacts the greatest rent which can be got for the use of his ground. (Smith, 1776 [1981]: 843)

Politics, in this model, complements economics, because of the way in which government raises revenue. Rent is the fulcrum point of the system. The land market is the mechanism that mediates between transport services and the competing uses and the preferences of users. The textbooks of 40 years ago, published as the planners were getting into their stride, were explicit on this:

> Because of the profit nature of their business, because of the travel time reduction, and because of a reduction in motor vehicle running cost … landowners can afford and do pay higher prices for the land than the current market price of the land before construction of the new highway. Thus this

higher price reflects the greater productivity of the land in its new use. (Winfrey, 1969: 498)

The changes in the net benefits accruing as a result of a new highway, according to the professor of civil engineering whom we have just quoted, could be anything of the order of an increase in land prices of 100 to 1,000 per cent. This was no mean transformation in the expectations of the community through which a highway penetrated. The pricing mechanism provided a precise index of the changes in benefits that the users expected to reap. One would have thought that this information was pertinent to the planners who were charged with guiding governments in the decisions about where, and how much, to invest. Land prices also said something about the distribution of windfall gains and people's capacity to pay for the new services – 'landowners may reap sizable windfalls from selling their land at these high prices brought on by the highway improvement. To such landowners their gain is unearned'. Even so, we are told, by the 1960s, 'All in all, land-value changes are not a part of economy studies for economic evaluation or project formulation of highway improvements ...' (ibid.: 499).

Was it this silence on the nature of rent which delivered the culture of statism that afflicts society today? If so, the problem is located in the financial architecture, and especially the state's role in failing to legitimise a distribution of income that reflected the economic potential of the industrial economy.

6   THE CULTURE OF STATISM

Counter-factual history

What if William Pitt had adopted Adam Smith's advice instead of introducing income tax in 1799? Might many of the social tensions and economic crises that befell Britain in the nineteenth century have been avoided? Scholars pose such questions to develop counter-factual history, an attempt to visualise how a community might have evolved if people had made decisions based on a wider range of choices. Historian Niall Ferguson (1997: 85) stresses that counter-factual scenarios are 'simulations based on calculations about the relative probability of plausible outcomes in a chaotic world (hence "virtual history")': 'Because decisions about the future are – usually – based on weighing up the potential consequences of alternative courses of action, it makes sense to compare the actual outcomes of what we did in the past with conceivable outcomes of what we might have done' (ibid.: 2).

To deny the possibility of alternative outcomes is to deny the state of freedom. Freedom consists in a person's right to choose how to live. To achieve that freedom, people need options, all of which must be realistic, some of which they must be free to sideline. Thus, it makes sense to ask: in the past, to what extent were people free to exercise the right of choice? Do systemic hurdles restrict people's choices today? How may we expand our options for the future?

In our view, the problems that confronted the pioneers of mass transport systems would have been nowhere near as horrendous if they could have captured more of the value they created. In fact, we postulate the probability that the relationship between the public and private sectors would have been altogether different if Parliament had followed Adam Smith's advice. We may see this in the current confusion over the status of Britain's rail network.

Economists at the Treasury and the Department for Transport, who sat in judgement on the financing arrangements of the privatised company, were outraged at the prospect of Railtrack paying £84 million in dividends to shareholders – a month before they were proposing to shut the company down. After all, wrote the then director of railways: 'Even after the assistance package last April [when Railtrack was advanced £1.5 billion], Railtrack declared a dividend. The company has clearly been badly managed since privatisation' (Osborne, 2005).

But weren't shareholders entitled to a return on the capital they had invested in Railtrack? Were the 'losses' attributable to operational inefficiencies or to the capital costs of renewing the rail infrastructure – and Parliament's failure to link capital investment with the ensuing value that spun off the tracks and into the pockets of landowners?

The failure to elaborate the accounts to identify all the value delivered by the railway enabled the Department for Transport to declare Railtrack commercially unviable. That brought privatisation to an end, and left investors holding shares that they could not sell.

Incoherence in the financial framework is disguised by the

government's follow-up experiment with the not-for-profit Network Rail. Its debt was forecast to reach over £13 billion by March 2004 (House of Commons Transport Select Committee, 2004: para. 80), and £23 billion by 2014. Nobody really knows whether the railways are financially viable or a noose around the nation's neck, because the Treasury fails to follow the money trail. It is appropriate to retrace our steps and take a closer look at the economics that confronted engineer George Stephenson.

The Stockton and Darlington Railway

Transport innovations open new frontiers even in old countries. They generate new commercial, social and psychological poss-ibilities. In Britain, the technologies eased access to the riches of nature that had been beyond reach. To exploit them, frontier towns were created, the grids of streets laid out across ancient fields to accommodate the influx of people who would extract the treasures that lay beneath the soil. Middlesbrough was one such town. It was established as a consequence of the founding of the Stockton and Darlington Railway. This strategy of extending the frontier, however, differed from the American model of colon-isation in one vital respect: the land had already been privatised by the aristocracy and gentry. Government could not offer free land as an inducement to investors to construct railways. Railway stockholders had to buy the land before they could lay a single mile of track. How did this affect railways and the economy of the United Kingdom?

The analytical starting point is the way in which a railway expands the production possibilities and therefore the value of enterprises. In the case of the most famous of the early railway companies, the one with which Stephenson was associated, the Stockton and Darlington Railway Company opened up 100,000 acres of coal which had previously been inaccessible.[1] Stephenson's railway slashed the costs of transportation from 7*d* per one ton of goods per mile on a wagon or by canal, to 1*d* on the railway. As a result, the price of coal fell by more than 6 shillings a chaldron (a unit of capacity equal to 36 bushels).

The postal service also enjoyed increased productivity. Its mail was carried at an astonishing 20 mph at one third of the former expense. This meant that, after the investors in the railway had made a profit, others would derive an additional material benefit based on a value that could be directly attributed to the railway's presence. In competitive conditions, that value could not be captured by the railway's investors. Who pocketed the difference?

The prospects of a railway were discussed for at least eight years up to 1818, as entrepreneurs ruminated over whether to favour a canal. Parliament rejected the railway proposal in 1819, but the enterprise received the royal assent in 1821. The backers included noblemen such as His Grace the Duke of Leeds, the Earls of Darlington and Strathmore, and Lords Dundas and Lascelles. They owned the land beneath which the rich seams of coal lay waiting. These landowners were well placed to derive a double windfall from the genius of people like Stephenson. First, the potential rent of their coal would be released. In addition, there was the rental value that would spill over into the general community. Thus, by monitoring the negotiations for the purchase of land on which to construct the railway, we derive an

---

1   This account of Middlesbrough and the Stockton and Darlington Railway is based on the primary materials – newspaper reports, leases, parliamentary debates and so on – conveniently compiled by Moorsom (1975).

impression of the measure of the heightened efficiencies achieved in the economy.

One beneficiary was the Bishop of Durham. His farmland was worth £5 an acre. Six acres were needed to construct the Middlesbrough branch line. The bishop's agent valued the land at £5,073 9s 3d. Because the valuation was contested, the purchase was placed before a jury in March 1829. William Jekyl, a bricklayer, valued the land at £3,876. The railway company had discharged him as an employee, dissatisfied with his work. Christopher Hunton valued the land at £3,161. 'There was an impression throughout the Court that this witness was drunk, but Mr. Coltman said it was merely a peculiarity of manner which he exhibited.' Thomas Farthing, publican, valued the land at £5,592. 'This witness admitted that he was fond of horse-racing, and indulged in speculative notions.' The valuations offered on behalf of the railway varied between £797 18s 11d and £1,107. In the event, reported the *Durham County Advertiser* (14 March 1829), the bishop was awarded £2,000, or £333 an acre. This was a massive increase in value derived not from a change in the intrinsic qualities of his acres, but because of the increased productivity that could be anticipated along the track between Stockton and the new town of Middlesbrough.

The *Durham Chronicle* of 1 January 1831 sang the praises of the railway, which

> has been productive of immense advantages to the
> neighbourhood through which the Railroad runs, by the
> facilities of conveyance which it has afforded to persons
> engaged in agricultural, commercial, manufacturing, and
> mining pursuits … [and] opening of a trade in coal between
> the London market and the various collieries contiguous to
> the Railroad. To effect this purpose, no expense or exertion

has been spared; and at length they have completed their
project, in a manner highly creditable to their own character
for enterprise and public spirit, and which promises to be
attended with the most beneficial and happy results to the
community at large.

Through the markets, part of the value of that 'enterprise and
public spirit' was siphoned into the pockets of the owners of land
for no good reason other than that they were the gatekeepers:
their permission was required to run the tracks over the land.

Before the branch line could be opened in December 1830,
the railway company had to buy more land at £322 an acre and
options to buy additional sites at £500 an acre. It was estimated
that in 1829 the savings arising from a reduction in the cost of
carrying coal amounted to £11,289.

The heightened economic activity also generated new business
for turnpike roads, whose tolls were increased; so much so that
their debts were discharged within five years after the opening of
the railway. The turnpikes became profitable even though they
lost the coal-carrying wagons. On those highways, one horse could
drag 1 ton at the rate of 8d or 9d a mile. On the railway, one horse
could draw 10 tons of coal at the rate of 3d per ton per mile. Those
net savings were converted into land values.

To open up the London trade, a new town would have to
be built at the mouth of the Tees, where the water was deep. A
consortium of investors purchased 1,040 acres from John Whin-
field Parrington. Joseph Pease sailed into the mouth of the River
Tees and landed on a spot where, from the mounds that were
etched into the landscape, he deduced ancient settlement. It was
here that they would break the ground and construct a new town.
He recorded in his diary:

> Imagination here had ample scope in fancying a coming
> day when the bare fields we were then traversing will
> be covered with a busy multitude and numerous vessels
> crowding to these banks denote the busy Seaport …
> Who that has considered the nature and extent of British
> enterprise commerce and industry will pretend to take his
> stand on this spot and pointing the finger of scorn at these
> visions exclaim, that will never be? … I believe it will. Had
> a most delightful sail on our return to Seaton calling and
> breakfasting at Cleveland Port, luxuriously entertained Tea
> Coffee Eggs Ham &c &c – 10d. each Waiter included.

The first 30 lots were auctioned at the Black Lion Hotel, Stockton, on 23 February 1830. To attract settlers, the advertisements promoted the properties as conveniently located just 150 yards from the new shipping facilities that were being constructed by the railway; enjoying a healthy, airy environment; and benefiting from beautiful views of the river and rural landscape. The streets were macadamised, and the town began to flourish, first relying on the trade hauled into town by the railway and then with the construction of an iron foundry in 1844.

Landowners made their fortunes. First, there were the rents from the extraction industries. Then, they protected their portfolios by offloading shares to urban investors who thought they could reap a profit from the fire-belching machines that were revolutionising the British economy. The railways, however, had accumulated debts, and someone would have to bear the loss.

The transport confidence trick

The flaw that nineteenth-century politicians built into the DNA of the British capitalist economy made inevitable the shift towards state penetration of commercial markets. That inevitability was not pre-determined, Marxist-style; but it was the logical outcome of the failure of fiscal policy.

In the vanguard of that process was the problem of funding the nation's infrastructure. In the nineteenth century, the unwitting losers were the people who invested in the capital projects – shareholders who lost their savings in the Great Capital Lock-up. Then, in the twentieth century, the losers became the taxpayers who were forced to assume responsibility.[2]

The shareholders of the early decades of industrialisation were entrapped in a process that was akin to a classic confidence trick.

The promoters of capital-intensive projects were vulnerable. They needed an escape plan. Timing was of the essence. They needed to execute their exit when the public believed that a project would deliver handsome dividends. Shares were sold when the price was at its highest. This enabled the promoters to recover their capital. The second generation of investors was saddled with debts that could not be funded out of revenue.

This process had two effects. First, it locked in the capital gains for the benefit of the promoters of the schemes. Second, it locked out the second wave of shareholders from dividends that they thought were in the offing.

No one warned investors that the financial rules were rigged against them. But the history of canal and railway construction

---

2   The state acquisition and/or funding of transport was *not* the outcome of a doctrinal preference, as under state socialism. It was inherent in the financial architecture of capitalism. Statism was well embedded in Britain before the landslide victory of the socialists after World War II. The Port of London came under public ownership in 1908. London Transport came into existence in 1933 and the British Overseas Airways Corporation in 1939 (Ricketts, 2005: 70).

ought to have alerted them against investing in transport unless they owned land. The distribution of risks and rewards is highlighted by the two models for extracting the net benefits from infrastructure.

The Bridgewater model

The risks were low for the Duke of Bridgewater, who pioneered canal building on his family estate. He captured the value that cascaded from the canal on to his land.

Such cases were not entirely risk free. An example was the Vend, a monopolistic organisation of collieries in the north-east that supplied coal to London. But new railways enabled other landowners to open seams that were previously inaccessible. The monopoly dissolved under the competition (Sweezy, 1938: ch. 10). Coal rents in the north-east declined, to resurface as increases in residential rents in London.[3]

The sucker model

Landowners would form a company to promote a railway. As their chairman they would often select their member of parliament. At an opportune time they sold their shares to merchants. The risks were transferred to urban investors, who were saddled with the debts arising from the investment in the infrastructure. The landowners 'cashed out' by suckering others into committing their savings, then retreating and capturing the rents that cascaded on to their land along the railway's route.

---

3   The breakdown of the Vend 'involved a transfer of income from the monopoly rent of the north eastern collieries to London users' (Hawke, 1970: 396).

Many shareholders, beguiled by the romance of steam and the publicity given to speculators who made fortunes, persisted with their investments.[4] The cumulative losses were enormous.

The sucker model was the practical option for the American West. Stewart Holbrook summarised the modus operandi. After the grant of a charter involving federal lands:

> Next the railroad boys would incorporate a land company, owned by directors of the railroad, to develop and peddle the lands. With the proceeds of the land sales, to which cash subsidies from Federal, state, or even city sources often were added, plus the sale of mortgage bonds in Europe, actual construction of the railroad was begun. Construction, however, was not done by the railroad company, but by a separate concern, also owned by the railroad's directors, which commonly paid off handsomely, although the grade was made and the rails laid at stupendous cost to the holders of the railroad's stocks and bonds. A considerable number of American railroads were financed by methods that cost the railroad's directors not a penny of their own in actual cash. (Holbrook, 1947: 154)

Why dilute a windfall fortune by carrying the costs of infrastructure when the risks can be shifted on to suckers?

But unless these funding loopholes are plugged, investors in the 21st century may shun future schemes. One of these is the alpine rail tunnel that France and Italy agreed to co-fund at a cost of €12.5 billion ($15.1 billion, £8.4 billion) in May 2004. The 52-kilometre tunnel will receive a contribution from Europe's taxpayers. But the two governments also want private investors to

---

4   The emergence of the limited liability company, which made access to small-value shares easy for urban savers, was cited by contemporaries as an encouragement to speculative investments (ibid.: 391).

bear 30 per cent of the cost. Should investors sink their savings into such a bore hole? The major windfalls will be reaped in the Italian province of Piedmont, where Turin is the capital. The tunnel is predicted to have an explosively beneficial impact on the regional economy. Italian Prime Minister Silvio Berlusconi drew attention to some of the benefits: the tunnel would halve freight time and costs and slash pollution levels. He forgot to mention that the net benefits would not seep into the wage packets of Fiat workers, but would surface as higher residential and commercial land values. Nor will the rents be shared with the taxpayers of the poverty-stricken southern regions of Italy, who will contribute to the government's share of the cost of the tunnel.

Rolling back the state

Funding infrastructure is a problem inextricably linked to the challenge of how to roll back the state's involvement in the economy. If we want to diminish the penetration of the state's activities in our individual lives, we first have to solve financial problems such as the funding of infrastructure.

The starting point for a reform agenda is the realisation that transport facilities do generate more than enough value to fund the capital beneath the wheels. In Britain the social rate of return on railway investment was between 15 and 20 per cent from 1830 to 1870, according to economic historian G. R. Hawke. This was, he explained, an underestimate:

> Investors in particular companies were probably correct
> in asserting that further expenditures by their companies
> were lowering their dividends. ... From a social point of
> view, the important implication is that the marginal social

rate of return was not declining between 1840 and 1870,
and that the rate of return remained above the likely rate on
alternative investments. (Hawke, 1970: 408)

Competition reduced the dividends paid to investors, but
economy-wide productivity rose. Enhanced gains ultimately
surfaced in the land market.

Social rates of return sum the total benefits to communities
throughout the nation. The economy gained from investment in
shipping and the iron industries, the increased efficiency in the
pooling and use of savings through innovations in the capital
markets, and from the expanding social and environmental
achievements that were delivered by the carriages on the iron
tracks. The economic, social and aesthetic gains translated into a
growing demand for land, and that raised rents to sums that were
at least equivalent to the capital cost of the railway revolution.

The problem for investors, however, was that the Irish navvies
who dug the earth out of the ground were shovelling money into
the pockets of landowners. The wheels delivered windfall fortunes
throughout the kingdom, but investors who were not landowners
were legally unable to claim a share. Although it was unable to
solve this problem, we will see mounting demands for the restoration of the state in the funding of utilities that were privatised in
the late twentieth century (as when the obsolescence of their infrastructure compels them to invest on a large scale). Eurotunnel,
once again, illustrates the point.

One million owners of shares in Eurotunnel sacked their board
of directors in April 2004 when their assets were deemed to be
almost worthless. They feared that they would lose their money
under the weight of the £6.4 billion debt. About 60 per cent of

the shares were in the hands of small investors in France, 5 per cent were held by the British public, and 10 per cent were owned by banks. In February 2004, Eurotunnel appealed for government intervention. It proposed a bail-out deal.

No one intended to dupe the investors who bought Eurotunnel shares. Their plight was the outcome of a financial architecture that separated the benefits of operating the tunnel from the benefits of owning land that was scattered throughout the nation. Small shareholders were not the original investors. Most of the institutions that financed or constructed the tunnel sold their shares when prices were at their peak. That locked in their gains, and shifted the risks to Johnny-come-lately savers. Rather than campaign for state aid, ought shareholders to engage in the search for a more efficient and fair funding model?

The challenge is to develop a win-win formula in which no one loses. Can this be achieved by the application of the principle that people should pay for the benefits they receive?

7 THE POLITICS OF ECONOMICS

Highways: waste not, want not

Trams, light trains that run on rails on roads, were the most economical, environment-friendly way to move people around towns. At their peak, 300 systems were operating in Britain. Then, in the late 1920s, tram companies began to capitulate in the face of two challenges. One was financial: the trams needed renewing, and the money was not available. The other problem was patronage. As Henry Ford's revolution spread to Europe, the cost of manufacturing automobiles was brought down. People sought the 'freedom of the road' with their own vehicles. Capitulation came in the 1960s, when Britain was left with a single tram. It ran along Blackpool's promenade for the benefit of tourists.

Freedom of the road came at a price. The open spaces in towns, and the arteries between towns, became increasingly valuable assets as people competed for their use. Pricing that space according to the rents that users would pay was the most efficient and fair way to conserve it. Pricing it was also the way to share it with others who could not afford automobiles. The rents from motorists could have been used to upgrade the trams. The outcome would have been an integrated strategy for highway mobility.

A financial discipline for the highways was imperative. Canals and railways were tightly contoured to the landscape, and they were economical in the use of land. Automobiles turned people into land-hungry travellers who could now wander almost anywhere. Roads had the potential to devour space, and they would do so if they were not disciplined by the pricing mechanism.

The economic case for integration has been thoroughly documented in the writings of Mason Gaffney. He stresses that the efficient use of land reduces the need for infrastructure. Compact cities reduce the length of highways and intensify the use to which we may put amenities such as sewerage, fire and police protection (Gaffney, 1964, 1969, 1970, 1972, 1973, 2001).

To achieve this outcome, people need to pay the competitive rate for the resources that they use. The beneficiaries should pay in proportion to the benefits that they derive. This is the principle applied in the private markets which we do not question when we buy a car or a pair of shoes. Similarly, the best results are achieved when the land market is free to operate efficiently by requiring beneficiaries to pay the rent that corresponds to the services they derive from the locations they occupy.

In automobile transportation, however, the tradition has been to treat time and space on our highways as free resources. The outcome is profligacy (see Box 6). But society, like nature, abhors a vacuum. The costs and benefits of the highways have to be registered in someone's profit-and-loss account. So if the people who invest in highway construction fail to recover the full value of the service they provide, the response is swift. The unclaimed value is internalised in other people's pockets! An example is the C$600m that was promised to upgrade the twisting Sea-to-Sky Highway that links Vancouver with Whistler, in British Columbia. The improvements were predicted to cut 30 minutes or more off the

Box 6 Efficiency gains from rental payments

Waste is built into people's habits when they are not obliged to pay rents. If rents are not factored into their profit-and-loss accounts, they enjoy subsidised lives at the expense of others. This is apparent in the attitudes of property owners in the commercial sector.

Freeholders, for example, who are not obliged to defray the cost of the services that they receive, may relax. One measure of this is the inefficient use of labour and capital. This finding emerged from an elegant piece of research by the Sir John Cass Business School in London. The accounts of 2,000 public companies were studied for every year between 1989 and 2002. The market value of companies that leased their properties (expressed as their share price) tended to far exceed their book values. The market valuation was based on the growth that they were expected to achieve. In other words, when they had to pay rent for the locational benefits they used, they had to take care of customers' interests.

The companies that owned the real estate they occupied, on the other hand – they did not have to pay rents – were not obliged to remain on their commercial toes. Their market value was closely aligned to their book value. The survey identified a strong correlation between leasing and sales growth. Companies with 100 per cent leased property reported annual increases in turnover of over 31 per cent. This contrasted with the 15 per cent rises for firms that owned their property (Jansen, 2003: 40).

two-hour drive. That was real value which, because the highway agency could not recover it to defray the construction costs, would be captured by others. The announcement of the investment was sufficient to raise property prices in communities along the route, such as Squamish (Warn, 2003). Land rose in value because the occupants knew they would not be invited to defray the costs of providing the added benefits for which they would be subsidised by the taxpayers of Canada. They would be the free riders who would reap the windfall.

An attempt has been made to quantify, on a global basis, the under-pricing of spatial resources used by road transport. In a global economy of $30 trillion, subsidies totalled $2 trillion, according to Professor Norman Myers. Road transport accounted for 48 per cent of all subsidies and 44 per cent of perverse subsidies ($640 billion a year):

> Car culture is most prominent in the US, supported by subsidies for both the oil and auto industries of $464 billion a year. Americans make 80 per cent of their trips by car whereas Europeans make 60 per cent of theirs by public transit, cycling or walking. The US price of gasoline is only three-quarters of Canada's and two-thirds of Australia's, yet these are both geographically large countries which supposedly requires extended auto driving. (Myers, 1999: 87)

The bold nature of the Myers study is marred by his failure to recognise that the market is not to blame. Problems that arise because people are not required to pay for the resources they use cannot be attributed to 'deficiencies of the market-place'. Those problems are the collateral consequences of the failure of public policy to partner the private pricing mechanism. This failure was emphatically illustrated by Arnold Schwarzenegger.

On 18 November 2003, the Hollywood star's first act on assuming the role of governor of California was to announce that he was reversing the proposal for a threefold increase in the car tax. The gas guzzlers of California who swallow the prairies were determined to pervert market economics in favour of an anti-market lifestyle. The prairies create the illusion of space in abundance. In fact, that space is finite. It is confined by the materials that are sunk into the surface. If motorists are not obliged to pay for the costs of the highways, they fill the space to congestion; and the negative consequences are imposed on others, as reflected in damage to the environment and to the fabric of communities.

Airways: appropriating the skies

For the builders of terrestrial transport systems, acquiring land was an expensive hurdle to overcome. No such problem ought to have arisen when mankind took to the skies, for the enclosers had not yet secured the title deeds to the heavens. If a problem did exist, this could not be attributed to private property or the markets. Here, then, we have a unique opportunity to identify the points of tension between transport systems, their funding and spatial location.

Defying gravity was the romantic heroics of Boy's Own comics. The Wright brothers led the pantheon of adventurers who turned Leonardo da Vinci's sketches into wood-and-steel frames that could be thrust above the ground. Individual displays of courage pepper the experiments in aerodynamics that enabled humans to compete with the birds for space among the clouds. The two bicycle mechanics who flew the first air machine in December 1903 heralded a new age by displaying the individual's imagination and willingness to risk all to push outwards the boundaries of human endeavour. But the advances in airways, culminating in the walk on the moon, were the product of the state.

In Britain, canals and railways were promoted by individuals who were backed by the risk capital of entrepreneurs. The aviation industry was sponsored by the state with taxpayers' money. The military potential of aircraft was developed in the Great War, and confirmed with strategic bombing raids in World War II. During the 1950s, state policy was developed to protect the flag carriers more as a matter of national prestige than of commercial interest.

In 1938, the US Federal Government developed a subsidy policy to protect private aviation enterprises during the formative stage of their development. Losses that arose as a result of 'honest, economical and efficient management' were to be defrayed by taxpayers. This policy was consolidated by the Air Co-ordinating Committee in Civil Air Policy (1954), which declared that foreign competition would prolong the need for public subsidies (Wassenbergh, 1957: 116). Europe's governments adopted a similar posture, extending the rationale for protecting the aviation industry by citing the need for economic growth.

The military implications of aircraft that could drop fire and damnation on the enemy inspired governments to channel resources into research and development (R&D) and the provision of aerodromes. Aviation ministries were established as arms of the state's bureaucracy. Empire-building rather than entrepreneurial activity was to the fore as money was poured into developing the science of aerodynamics. Even privately owned enterprises were regarded as of state significance, as nurseries for the training of pilots whose services would be needed in wartime. The private sector's progress was in the form of spin-offs from military applications, as in the Boeing 707, which metamorphosed out of a flight refuelling tanker for the B-52 bomber.

Most airports were owned by municipalities. After World War II, in Britain, many of those aerodromes were acquired by central government with the intention of establishing a national airports system. In the event, many of them were returned to municipal control until privatisation began in the 1980s. But privatisation did not bring with it a complete programme based on the principles of commercialisation. Government mentality remained locked in the planner's paradigm.

With the creation of BAA plc, a new regime of regulation and charges was established. These were not based on the market principle of charging as much as the market would bear: allowing the willing customer to pay for the benefit of landing and picking up passengers and cargo. A similar policy void was evident elsewhere in the world. Planners were more concerned with physics than with the fisc. Landing charges were related to the weight of the craft and the damage it inflicted on the runway rather than the rent generated by the demand for the time-and-space slots above airports. The economics of the market took a back seat to the engineering values in which the planners were schooled.

Additions to weight-related landing charges included passenger service charges, but the commercialisation of the privatised airlines was not matched with an equal concern to optimise either the pricing regime or the revenue of the state. The outcome, by default, was the privatisation of time and space above airports. Airlines asserted 'grandfather' rights in the resources of the heavens as they exploited the failure of government to enforce the proprietary interests of the nation on behalf of taxpayers who had financed the industry in the first place.

This fiscal failure did not stem from a reluctance to engage in the terms on which airlines and passengers might use airports. A veritable army of consultants was mustered to measure noise and the emission of pollutants so that surcharges might be imposed. The scope for controversy over environmental and social issues was endless, leading to arbitrary charges based, ultimately, on either subjective values or political expediency.

Government and privatised airlines evolved a self-serving tangle of regulations that conspired to confuse passengers. Airports now have more in common with shopping malls than aerodromes. The profits from renting retail space enable airport owners to claim that they are profitable enterprises, even though they fail to charge the full market rents for the right to use their runways. The result is a distorted pricing regime and the guerrilla warfare in which lobbyists engage to preserve vested interests. This helps to obstruct a coherently integrated network of roadways, railways, airways and waterways.

The history of state sponsorship is now cited as evidence against the deregulation and privatisation of the airline industry (Reed, 2002). In public policy terms, the origin of airways is significant, but not necessarily for the reasons favoured by those who oppose market economics. Unfortunately, the debate between those who favour state regulation, and their opponents who favour markets, continues to be conducted in the conceptual categories of the past century when capitalism and socialism were locked in mortal combat. The epistemological damage inflicted by that doctrinal contest was profound. It bequeathed a language that concealed a more complex reality, one that, had it been correctly excavated, might have led to a negotiated settlement between ideological enemies.

An enormous economic value was created as a result of the state's investment in aircraft technology. That investment could not be obstructed by the costs of access to the sky, for the state claimed eminent domain over the heavens above its territory. The rents of the skies belonged to the nation. So when the time came to privatise airlines and airports, it was incumbent on governments to ensure a smooth transition to the correct combination of pricing and property rights. They failed to show due diligence and deprived their citizens of the financial rewards that would flow from tapping the rents of the skies. That, in turn, created barriers to entrepreneurship and the investment of private capital in the airline industry. So today the privatised industry of the 21st century is confronted by a legacy of regulatory and financial practices that constrains its performance.

A sense of the scale of the problem was identified by Sir Rod Eddington, who censured American bankruptcy laws that protected inefficient airlines. Speaking in September 2005, he declared in his final speech as chief executive of British Airways: 'In the last four years, the US airlines have soaked up $15 billion to $20 billion (£8.3 billion to £11 billion) of public subsidies and loan guarantees. They're operating in protected markets, they're hoovering up public funds and still they can't make a profit' (quoted in Boxell, 2005).

The dispute between the EU and the US government over subsidies to their respective aircraft makers stems from their commitment to a dysfunctional 'business model', the costs of which ultimately fall on taxpayers. If new approaches on land, water and in the skies are not developed based on rolling back the power of the state, we may anticipate further deterioration of productivity in the sector committed to private enterprise.

The corruption of enterprise

We have established that, in the nineteenth century, the enterprise economy was not constructed on integrated foundations. Because the pricing mechanism was compromised, enterprises (and the ownership of capital itself) were ultimately vulnerable to state control. In the fate of the canal we may observe the embryonic forces that nurtured the corruption of enterprise. By failing to provide the legal and institutional framework for optimal pricing, Parliament fostered a legacy in which choices were increasingly narrowed even as science and technology were expanding people's options. The ethics of individualism and communalism were compromised in favour of authoritarian collective structures. Thus were sown the seeds for the emergence of twentieth-century statism and welfare dependency. There were four stages in this unfolding drama.

Stage I: eighteenth-century canals

The state was not equipped to intervene in private enterprise. Its bureaucratic and legislative capacities would need to develop before government could entertain the idea of nationalising a major enterprise. The state had hitherto relied on freebooters as its economic extension of the political structure, notably on the high seas. So when investors in canals found that they were locked into debts that deprived them of dividends, subsidies from taxpayers were not an option. The fate of the Leominster Canal illustrated the risks of sinking one's savings into infrastructure.

Britain was swept by canal mania in the early 1790s. Excavations across the landscape appeared to be money-making ventures, and the Leominster project in Herefordshire was one speculative outcome. The nearby coal deposits could be tapped for consumers in Ludlow and Leominster. An engineer was hired, a consortium of investors assembled and the first seven boat-loads extracted from the land of Sir Walter Blount were towed from Marlbrook to Woofferton in 1794. Two years later a second Act of Parliament was passed to authorise the issue of a further £180,000 capital, and in that year the entire section between Leominster and the Marlbrook wharves was completed. Fourteen boat-loads of Sir Walter's coal halved the wharf price at Leominster on the first day.

Fifty years later, the owners of the canal viewed the impending competition from railways as a mixed blessing. The proprietors wanted to be bought out because the canal had

> absorbed vast sums of capital without payment of a single penny of dividend to its subscribers. The proprietors, having seen the writing on the wall, must then have awaited the impending railways and positively welcomed the prospect of any railway encroachment on their territory – as seemingly the only likely escape from their financial difficulties. (Calderbank, 2001: 1)

Success or failure? In the 60 years of its operations, the canal failed to pay dividends. Was this venture, then, a reckless one from its inception? The truth is, we cannot tell without an accounting of all the benefits generated by the canal, including those that were not shown in its profit-and-loss accounts. To brand the canal a commercial loss is premature, because some of the value it generated was 'off balance sheet'.

First, there were the acres from which the coal was extracted. Without the canal, those deposits would have remained worthless. Landowners such as Sir Walter of Sodington Hall enriched themselves with the rents that were made possible by the canal. We have it on the authority of Adam Smith that the likes of Sir Walter would not have leased out their coal deposits if they had not been induced to do so with the offer of rent. Referring to coal mines in Scotland, Smith (1776 [1981]: 182) noted that 'the landlord will allow nobody else to work them without paying some rent'.[1]

A second source of externalised value was the increased productivity achieved in locations such as Ludlow and Leominster. Amazing things happened when you brought a horse to water:

> A pack-horse could move, perhaps, one eighth of a ton.
> The same animal could move five-eighths of a ton by stage
> wagon on soft roads, but 30 tons by river barge and as much
> as 50 tons when dragging a narrow boat along a canal with
> no current. It is clear that the advent of the inland canals
> was indeed a transport revolution. (Heatley, 2000: 395)

The dramatic reduction in the cost of coal increased the disposable incomes of the town dwellers. The benefits did not remain with the wage earners, however. Through the competition for access to residential properties in the catchment area of a canal's wharves, landlords were able to raise the rents of dwellings. Because the price of coal was reduced people could afford to pay higher rents.

The canal made a majestic contribution to the economy of this part of the English Midlands near the Welsh border. So it would be premature to pronounce the Leominster Canal a commercial loser. But because of competition, and in the absence of a mechanism for recycling back into the canal some of the rents it generated, some investors were bound to lose. They were the

---

1   The Blounts worked some of the coal deposits themselves and leased out others until they ceased direct participation in the extraction of coal in 1868.

shareholders who responded to the 1791 Act of Parliament and contributed to the capital that was needed to acquire land and employ the navvies to dig the channel along which the coal would be transported.

The winners were the shareholders, who, although they did not receive a dividend, benefited from the rents of their coal deposits. Among them was Sir Walter, a prominent member of the founding committee. These investors could write off the capital they sank into the canal as part of the costs of exploiting coal deposits. But because of the structure of property rights, canal shareholders who were not landowners could not claim part of the coal rents. Parliament, for its part, saw no reason to sanction a mechanism that would enable all investors to benefit from the value they helped to create. Thus, Parliament sponsored a new system for transferring wealth from the investors in companies to the owners of land. The nation's financial architecture was one gigantic wheel for rolling value away from those who created it to those who happened to have their names on the title deeds of land.

The Leominster Canal survived until 1847. By then, railways had made their appearance. The shareholders solicited a deal with the Shrewsbury and Hereford Railway in the hope of recovering part of their capital. Whether the canal was self-funding depends on the total value that accrued to the landowners in its catchment area. No accounting convention was available to enable investors to reach a conclusion on that question. In the event, the Shrewsbury and Hereford Railway paid £12,000 for the canal's assets in 1857, and the canal was closed down a year later.

The financial logic that underpinned the canals was designed to part people from their money, but were the promoters aware that they were luring dupes into investing in enterprises from which they could not receive a square deal? Landowners like Sir Walter recovered part of their capital by selling their shares to cash-rich urban merchants. Theirs was a double-take. First, they reaped the rents from their estates. Then, they made super-profits from the sale of canal shares during the boom times. The losers, caught up in the spells of mania, did not realise that they were walking into a financial trap.

Stage II: nineteenth-century railways

The same financial process played itself out in the railway sector. Small investors found themselves as vulnerable as those who had sunk their savings into canals. The financial model sanctioned by Parliament failed to buttress the enterprise economy, but it would be another century before the state, drawing on its successful engagement in World War II, felt confident enough to assume ownership of the industry and bail out the shareholders.

When a Labour government took control of Britain's railways, it was possible for socialists to claim that 'the significant thing is that the railways were not paying their way when nationalised' (Labour Research Department, 1950: 81). They appeared to have a case. In 1938, the last complete year before wartime government control of the network, three railway companies with over £200 million of ordinary stock paid no dividends. Great Western paid 0.5 per cent on its £43 million ordinary stock. The analysis, however, was partial, characterising 'the basic problem' as being the difference between the rates the railways charged their customers and the prices they had to pay for labour and raw materials. This was a crude accounting. If a railway's productivity included value that was beyond the reach of the rates it could charge, that value nonetheless had to be imputed if a correct financial portrait of commercial viability was to be developed. This was not done in time to save the nation's railways from the clutches of a state that now believed it knew how to run a railway.

Stage III: twentieth-century highways

The state had the opportunity to learn from earlier mistakes. The economics of the new age of mobility were understood by the Liberal politicians who rose to power at the turn into the twentieth century. They knew that as the costs of mobility came down, the value of highway space went up. So it made sense to use those rents to upgrade highway surfaces and fund trams for people on lower incomes. Surfaces would have to be relaid with more durable materials and the roads would have to be widened. Political leaders and the emerging automobile industry accepted that the capital cost ought to fall on those who would reap the windfall gains.

In the Public Street Works Acts of the 1890s, the cost of paving urban streets was laid on the owners of land.[2] The construction industry appreciated that the added value which spilled over into land values would have to be recycled into the infrastructure. This economic insight was not lost on Liberal MPs, one of whom was the author Hilaire Belloc. He was commissioned by the British Reinforced Concrete Engineering Co. to study the highways of England. Belloc proposed a national

---

2   This fiscal philosophy was applied in the waterlogged region of East Anglia in the 1920s. The cost of draining the fens was placed on landowners in the vicinity, under the Land Drainage Acts.

fund to finance a network of highways that would internalise part of the added value:

> The grant of new roads should include the purchase, if not of a continuous belt along each side, at least of blocks of land, especially in the neighbourhood of existing communications, near railway stations, near villages or other centres now established, etc. the price to be determined by arbitration upon the old price basis before the scheme of the Road was developed. If this were done the great difficulty for certain purposes (not residential, but other) of using these sites would accrue to the public purse and would gradually relieve the cost of construction. (Belloc, 1923: 204)

Belloc argued that the landowner should not pocket the benefit: compensation should be based on existing values, rather than those that would arise from the enhanced productivity delivered by a new highway. The reservation of land 'on either side of the way for the purpose of helping to pay for the new scheme would be of direct advantage to the community and of disadvantage to no one'. Without such a funding model, the nation would 'make a direct and immediate present of millions to the chance owners of land upon their trajectory. It would be a gross case of actual endowment at the expense of the community' (ibid.: 204–5).

Landowners, through the House of Lords, resisted the logic of this plan. The Liberal government of 1905–10 attempted to formalise the philosophy in the nation's budget, but policy was skewed to accommodate the fact that 'the landed interest [feared] it would lose the benefit it could expect from the growth of road transport in a consequent increase in land values' (Hibbs, 1982:

47). Parliament was not to be allowed to integrate the financial system at the interface between private users and social spaces.

Stage IV: 21st-century space travel

Governments, repeating the errors and omissions of the terrestrial age, failed to secure the correct configuration of property rights and payments for the space age. Instead, they subsidised both the airline industry and the corporations that benefit from the rents of the satellites in geo-synchronous orbit around earth. The failure to charge sky rents will one day emerge as serious as the financial problems that afflicted investors in canals and railways.

Pricing amenities in social spaces

Public and private finances are interlocked. Unless we adopt Adam Smith's financial template, we will not be able to develop an integrated transport system. The looming crisis in Britain's rail industry accentuates the urgency of the need for new directions in fiscal policy.

Train operating companies have warned that overcrowding on some routes will become intolerable by 2015 (Association of Train Operating Companies, 2005). Under the current financial model, they are led to recommend the closure of some stations and a hike in fares to squeeze out some of their prospective passengers. Overcrowding will become even more acute if Britain does shift to a road pricing policy that persuades some motorists to travel by train.

The shortfall in the quality of the amenities provided by railways is matched by the shortfall in funds. The 'funding gap' is predicted to shrink from £4.9 billion a year to £2.2 billion in the years up to 2015, but an increase in revenues may not be the best outcome. A flexible fare regime that reflects the costs of peak-time travel, for example, would be desirable; but the problem remains with the upgrading of the infrastructure. The train operators appear to be pessimistic about the prospects of expanding the network to keep pace with demand – and to reduce the pressure on highways. And yet, that is precisely where the debate should be focused: on funding improvements to the tracks that take the wheels that create the fortunes. Otherwise, a pricing squeeze on motorists will not be offset by a diminishing fare structure on the railways.

This is not a uniquely British problem. The integration of the European economy is likely to be prejudiced unless the funding problem is resolved. To gain the benefits of an expanded domestic market, the eastern European countries that were admitted to EU membership in May 2004 must upgrade their communications networks. They hope that private capital will come to their aid, but they are not able to offer the state guarantees that are sought by investors (Anderson, 2004). Should such guarantees be necessary? The size of the domestic capital markets in countries like Poland need not constrain the provision of infrastructure. EU governments could reform taxes in favour of the self-funding model. This would yield a double dividend. The eastern Europeans would rebuild their infrastructure, while encouraging people to save and invest in domestic businesses that create jobs and marketable products.

The economics of the new financial strategy were succinctly noted by *Financial Times* columnist Samuel Brittan. There could be no 'valid free market objection to taxing pure increases in land value if this can be done without unintentionally taxing enterprise too' (Brittan, 2003). The challenge for Europe's statesmen is to shift the structure of taxes so that the 'social opportunity costs' are progressively reduced.

The democratic debate, however, needs to reach beyond purely economic considerations. Personal liberty and the vitality of communities are of equal concern – and integral to the character of the free market. We may approach these broader issues in terms of one of the objections to road pricing. We are warned that Big Brother would track us through the satellites connected to the black boxes in our cars. Is this an intrusion into our personal space? In a strong sense, the answer must be in the affirmative. And if we did not approach this question in a comprehensive way, the libertarian objection might carry force. But it has to be qualified in at least two ways.

First, the individual on a highway is occupying a social space. It is not the motorist's space. At best, the traveller is renting the time and place between two points on a journey. Social obligations attach to the opportunity, for which the individual is answerable. Hitherto, the individual has not been able to fulfil his obligations (as with pollution of the environment, which is an intrusion on other people's right to a healthy atmosphere). Rebalancing rights and responsibilities with respect to the use of social space must form part of the fiscal reform agenda.

Compensating for that intrusion, however, would be the reduction in Big Brother's engagement in our personal lives through the taxes that are currently levied. Citizens are subject to the most draconian inspection of their persons and property. They have to account to the Inspector of Taxes in minute detail for their affairs. Most of that intrusion can be eliminated by the simple expedient of retiring the bad taxes that are levied on earned incomes and savings.

This adjustment of the structure of public finance both emancipates the individual and liberates the market economy to deliver on its historic promise – prosperity for all who are willing to work, save and invest. But this can be achieved only if governments rely more on pricing the use of amenities that are accessed through the common spaces in our communities. The social dividends, as we shall now see, would be enormous.

8 ACCOUNTING FOR DEMOCRATIC GOVERNANCE

The First Law of Social Dynamics

If we accept the Treasury's measure of the damage it causes to the economy (30p/£), Britain lost £120 billion in wealth and welfare as a result of the taxes it levied in 2003/04 (£399 billion) (HM Treasury, 2005: table C8), rising to a loss of about £138 billion in 2005/06. This value exceeds the funds required to provide all the *additional* services the nation needs. These sums are underestimates of the real sacrifice made by the nation. Nonetheless, they represent a loss of about £1 trillion during the lifetime of the Blair government's search for value for money from public services.

The cumulative deficit in the wealth of the nation over the two centuries since 1799, when Parliament first adopted income tax, is the measure of the persistent failure of public finance policies. Our quest is to specify strategies that are sustainable in the context of the way we achieve mobility in a fast-moving world.

Our self-funding 'sustainable' mobility hypothesis may be contrasted with the idea of perpetual motion, which was first conceived by Indian mystics in the twelfth century. During the Enlightenment, artists and philosophers searched for the secret of the costless way to drive vehicles. Leonardo da Vinci sketched a self-moving car. It was a futile project. Perpetual motion would subvert the laws of nature. The dreamers were seeking to violate the First Law of Thermodynamics, which states that energy cannot be created or destroyed. Costless mobility was a fantasy. Even so, we can move closer to the notion of perpetual motion than the current approaches to mobility, which are wantonly profligate with energy, space and the demands on our lives.

The closest we can come to perpetual motion is the financial formula that I call the First Law of Social Dynamics. The law concedes that motion will consume energy, but the benefits are maximised for the least possible input of time, energy and space. *The mechanism that drives this law of social behaviour and organisation is the requirement that those who wish to enjoy mobility should defray the costs by paying for the benefits.* They should provide the resources to keep the wheels turning. Free riders are not welcome. This disciplines consumption, and the operating mechanisms become self-sufficient in the sense that their costs are not transferred to people who do not benefit from them.

The law operates within the framework of free markets. The mechanics of the process are well established. They start with the capacity of markets to value accurately the net benefits of mobility. The self-funding principle requires an open, interdependent system. A railway or highway remains viable only for so long as it is wanted by the users who are willing to pay for the mobility it generates: that is, only for so long as it adds value to the individual's and the community's wealth and welfare. To be viable it has to be integrated into the needs of the public it serves.

But the valuation of land, which is crucial to the self-funding system, is alleged by critics to be a problem. This is spurious. London would not have achieved world-class status in the twentieth century if its transport providers had believed that.

The builders of London's commuter trains had no difficulty

in measuring the value of land or, on occasion, capturing it. Notable was the testimony of Frank Pick (1878–1941), a solicitor who joined the North Eastern Railway in 1902. He was hired by the Underground Group in 1907, and he played a crucial role in the evolution of the capital's transport network over the next 30 years. As vice-chairman of the London Passenger Transport Board he highlighted the significance of land values in evidence to the Barlow Commission:[1]

> The moment an underground extension is projected the value of the land is at least doubled. When the railway is built and the stations are opened the land adjacent to the stations is at least quadrupled in value … In view of the difficulty of maintaining a public utility like the London Passenger Transport Board in a satisfactory condition from the receipts of fares there is every reason, in the interests of the public, why the Board should receive its appropriate share of the land values it helps to create … The earnings of a Tube railway, even under favourable circumstances, are not sufficient to provide the interest and the sinking fund upon the capital invested. (Quoted in Halliday, 2001: 104)

The Metropolitan Railway financed investment by buying green fields to the north of London, at agricultural prices, and capitalising on the rise in the value that was fostered by the arrival of their trains. Pick believed that this model should be adopted for further investment in London's Underground. He was to be disappointed: 'This potentially valuable source of railway finance was once again not taken up. Profits from property development

---

1   The Royal Commission on the Geographical Distribution of the Industrial Population (1939), known as the Barlow Commission after its chairman, Sir Montague Barlow.

would go only to property developers. The benefit to railway companies would be confined to the extra journeys of those who travelled to and from the properties' (quoted in ibid.: 104). Handing the value created by the Underground trains to others subverted the financial viability of transport services. It dissipated the value that was needed to ensure the continuous upgrading of infrastructure.

While there are methodological challenges with respect to dividing rent into its component parts (what part may be attributed to the good local school compared with access to the subway station?), there is no merit in the claim that it is difficult to separate the value of land per se from buildings.

In Japan, the Ministry of Land, Infrastructure and Transport notes that their 'land is regarded as a separate asset from buildings' (Ministry of Land, Infrastructure and Transport, 2002: para. 1). The compilation of statistics on land values throughout the nation is comprehensive.

Denmark has levied a charge on land values for the past 80 years, with no practical difficulties in valuing land for fiscal purposes (Lefmann and Larsen, 2000).[2] Similar conclusions apply to the administration of land taxation in New Zealand and Australia.[3]

If governments are serious about privatising transport services and removing capital costs from their books, they will need to cooperate with entrepreneurs and civic communities in the quest

[2]   The British Treasury appears to be impressed by the evidence on the Danish land tax (see HM Treasury, 2003: box 2.12, p. 122). The practical, neighbourhood-level reappraisal of land values in Denmark was cheap to administer and it attracted few appeals (see Müller and Mørch-Lassen, 1989).

[3]   Australia's valuation expertise may be assessed by reviewing the website of the Valuer General of New South Wales. See www.lands.nsw.gov.au.

for solutions. This entails the search for practical policies in place of political rhetoric.[4] Fashionable concepts like sustainability need to be translated into functional mechanisms. By harnessing the power of the First Law of Social Dynamics, problems may quickly be resolved. Two examples illuminate the point.

In Europe, disputed ownership rights over the time and space above airports will continue to disfigure the airline industry. Lower-fare airlines are seeking greater access to major airports like Paris Orly. They are resisted by squatters, the flag carriers that inherited their slots from the state without obligation to pay the full market rent. One outcome was estimated by the London-based consultancy National Economic Research Associates. The EU's 20 most crowded airports could accommodate 52 million more passengers a year by 2007 if the landing slots were placed on a commercial footing (Walsh, 2004). The consultants suggested that the slots should be publicly traded so that they were reallocated to those who could fly full plane loads. Absent from this proposal, however, was consideration of ownership rights. If these were retained in the public domain, the efficient market policy would be annual rental charges that soaked up the full potential, determined by auctions (as in Hong Kong), matched by commensurate reductions in taxes.

Back on earth, carnage on the roads is the human price that is paid for the failure to employ optimum pricing policies. According to the World Health Organisation and the World Bank, road traffic accidents are likely to become the world's third-biggest cause of death and disability by 2020. Road crashes kill 1.2 million people every year and injure 50 million more. Deaths from traffic

---

4   This point was forcefully put by *Financial Times* columnist John Plender (2004).

accidents will increase by 80 per cent in the developing countries by 2020 (Williams, 2004). Investment in safer, more efficient forms of mobility is required, but the funds for these are said to be in short supply. But the World Bank fails to commend the self-funding strategies; or it does so in a tepid way, as in the case of privatisation policies in the Philippines.

While urging the need to reduce dependence on government finance in favour of private investment, the World Bank merely alludes to optimal funding policies. It acknowledges that property developers would invest in improved transport amenities 'to maximise the value of their land and property holdings and to secure air rights to the space over and around stations and terminals for commercial and retail development' (World Bank, 2000: 67). But from where would the funding come to defray the capital costs? The World Bank waits until its last sentence to meekly suggest that consideration be given to the possibility that 'landowners speculating on real estate appreciation [might] contribute to right-of-way costs' (p. 68). Such timidity in analysis gives comfort to politicians who prefer not to appear intellectually adventurous.[5]

Has the time come for a principled approach that fits with the commercial model? Should people pay for the benefits they receive? With the leaders of the G8 countries urging developing nations to improve governance in return for debt relief, we may judge Western governments by similar criteria.

---

5   How to transform the virtues of democracy (transparency and accountability) into a political problem is illustrated by the treatment of public charges on land values by Klaus Deininger (2003). The high visibility of the charges, he claims, 'makes their introduction more difficult' (p. 168); not least because of the 'political clout of landlords' (p. 169). World Bank pessimism is infectious, especially among politicians in need of campaign funds.

Paying for benefits received

Few of the members of the British Chambers of Commerce (10 per cent of them) accept that transport fully meets their needs. Indeed, the ability to expand their enterprises was hindered by transport infrastructure (39 per cent). So what did they think about the funding issue? They were informed that 'Significant increases in property prices are often associated with new local transport initiatives, for example the Jubilee Line London tube extension'. Would they support the proposal that some of that increase should be reinvested in transport? Compared with 19 per cent who favoured that policy, 54 per cent opposed it (British Chambers of Commerce, 2004).

Most property owners wanted to pocket the windfalls. That meant others would have to pay for the capital investment which they wanted to use. But what if reform included reductions in those taxes that damaged the interests of themselves and their tenants? That would expand their markets and the communities in which they lived would be renewed. That richer prospectus, I suggest, would attract the support of most of them.

A pact between people and property is needed, built around a trade-off: lower taxes for a commitment to earmark rents to fund shared services. This was the message of London property developer Don Riley, whose book *Taken for a Ride* (2001) contributed significantly to the public debate in Britain on how to harness location rents to fund infrastructure. London property owners, including the City of London, should take the lead in showing government that measuring and valuing land and recycling incremental values into community services is a practical proposition. Riley explains how, with the aid of a slide rule and some basic information on the footprint of a property, owners or their agents can easily measure the land area of each of their properties. So instead of floor-by-floor assessments, owners, aided by people with local knowledge, would place their individual properties into a banded scale of site values. Colour-coded banding on land maps would quickly reveal sites that were over- or under-valued. In Riley's case, 'If we were to levy my location at £2 a square foot, on a current land value of £250 a square foot, the location levy would be the equivalent of £124,000 a year. A 10-year levy for transport revitalisation would ensure that my location values were enhanced to perhaps £350 per square foot.'

The traditional landed class might resist this proposal. But we may appeal to their self-interest, to recognise that their London estates would gain from the restructuring of taxation. They do not travel by public transport but thanks to the tax system we may say that they top the list of free riders. They must appreciate that they have a stake in funding London's transport system out of rents. Through the Crown Estate, for example, the Queen is now spending £500 million on reconstructing parts of Regent Street. The Crown Estate will need shoppers to throng into the West End, but people with discretionary cash to spend are likely to boycott the antiquated Underground facilities that most commuters have to use. But by upgrading the ambience of travel on the Tube, making travel into Piccadilly Circus and Oxford Street a pleasure, the rents of the Crown Estate would be boosted.

But there would be a price: the commitment by government to abolish taxes that damage the economy. Capital gains and inheritance taxes, for example, may be abolished and income tax rates reduced to make way for public charges on the rents of land.

The transition to the new arrangements would be politically

attractive because, in the early stages, spending on shared services would not be reduced. Equivalent sums would be raised through the levy on land values (Riley, 2003). This would ensure the continuity of the services people need while affording them time to taste the benefits of the reform.

Elements of the new strategy are already emerging.

The 3G electromagnetic spectrum auction generated £22.4 billion for the Treasury in 2000. The telecom operators were willing to bid that much for the privilege of holding 20-year licences, which was the market's valuation of the rents of the radio spectrum (Harrison, 2003).

Renting the use of valuable space is accepted as the solution to congestion. London's congestion charge is crude yet effective in reducing congestion and pollution.[6] More than a dozen cities are interested in following the capital's example, and the government is proposing electronic 'tagging' in cars which will register from 2p per mile on quiet roads to £1.30 per mile on busy roads at peak times.

Transport for London and transport agencies elsewhere are proposing that they should have the right to borrow money from

---

6   Rana Roy (1998) points out that congestion charging is equivalent to premium rents on residential and commercial space in central urban areas and that 'this practice is accepted as a natural solution by all parties – by economists, politicians, residential and commercial tenants, and the public at large' (p. 56). If congestion charging were applied uniformly throughout Britain the result would be a financial surplus of around £10 billion – five times the level of public subsidies to rail at the time he was writing. The striking difference between the rents of roads and urban residential and commercial space, however, was obvious. The latter is 'owned by a small minority of property owners. The premium prices ... accrue to this minority. (Nor are they recycled back to the tenants or to society at large.) In contrast, we, the public, own the roads. Hence, any premium prices paid by passengers and freight users in an efficient pricing regime would, in the first place, accrue to all of us'.

the capital markets (offering the future stream of fare revenue as security), but more importantly that they be granted the use of financial instruments to tap land values that were enhanced by transport investment. Some entrepreneurs from the transport and property sectors endorse Bob Kiley's stress on the need for new infrastructure because 'Business cannot make important investment decisions while there is uncertainty about future transport plans' (Sheppard et al., 2003). They propose that part of the property tax that they pay on their commercial premises should be ring-fenced for transport.

There are many sources of economic rents to be tapped to enhance the performance of both private commerce and public services.[7] Using these to pay for shared services, however, is not an extension of conventional tax philosophy: it is based on the principle that people pay directly for the benefits that they choose to receive by virtue of the locations they choose to occupy. Can we afford not to deepen fundamental reform? The scale of the gains is made apparent by a comprehensive audit of the costs of funding transport out of taxes.

Accounting for leakages and losses

Treasury accounting conventions conceal information that ought to be in the public domain. The issue of transparency may be considered in relation to the revival of plans to construct Crossrail, the rival to the Jubilee Line in the 1980s.

Funding, as ever, was the obstacle to a vital addition to the capital's rail network. Mayor Livingstone's consultants argued

---

7   For an extensive list of these non-distorting sources of revenue, see Gaffney (1998).

ACCOUNTING FOR DEMOCRATIC GOVERNANCE

that the £7 billion cost could be more than justified. The total of £19 billion benefits came from additions to output associated with increased accessibility to central London, including £8 billion from savings in journey times. This gain, suggested the mayor, could be achieved by funding Crossrail by the following means:

- 'Roughly half' could come from taxes – say, £3.5 billion (Livingstone, 2004);
- £2 billion from 'predicted rises in land values along the route' (Blitz, 2004).
- £1.5 billion from an increase in Tube and bus passengers' fares.

A return of £19 billion over a 30-year period against the investment of £7 billion appears to be a good deal, but the bottom line is not so generous when we factor in the losses and leakages.

The cost of the Treasury's £3.5 billion must be adjusted to take account of the deadweight loss. The Treasury favours a cautious 30p/£ ratio, but other economists have suggested estimates ranging from 50p to £1.50 for every £1 raised by bad taxes. If we split the difference and assume that the loss is £1, the cost of public investment in Crossrail doubles to £7 billion. But if we want to appreciate the true scale of the impact of taxes on Britain, we need to adjust that cost even further.

According to the most recent research, by Professor Nicolaus Tideman, tax-induced losses are potentially as high as £2 for every £1 raised with the aid of 'bad' taxes (see Box 7). If this is correct, the cost of Crossrail to taxpayers rises from £3.5 billion to more than £10 billion. If we add to this the costs of the inequities arising

Box 7 **The historic reality**

Treasury economists treat the deadweight loss of taxes by taking the economic system as it exists. This means that their measure of the social opportunity cost of taxpayers' money ignores the additional value that would be generated if taxation were as efficient as it would be if government employed Adam Smith's fiscal recommendations.

In particular, the losses arising from inefficiencies in the land market (through land hoarding and under-use) are ignored. These losses must be attributed to the tax system, because they would not be incurred if people had to pay rent for the benefits delivered to their land. Owners would not keep their sites idle or under-used, as many of them do at present. Taking this into account, the estimate of losses arising from the present tax regime would rise by a significant factor.

Viewing the losses as potential gains under the optimum fiscal/pricing system is reasonable. The losses are the result of economic attrition that has been going on for two centuries. Reversing that history would take time, of course; so the immense gains would also take time to percolate through, as the economy adjusts to higher levels of productive efficiency.

from the leakages of value into the land market, the benefits of Crossrail are wiped out.[8]

The accounting deficiencies may be further illuminated on a national scale by the Blair government's ten-year transport plan.

---

8   We have not begun to trace the consequences of the leakages that drive people out of employment, forcing them into dependency on the public purse and thereby imposing further costs on taxpayers.

When it was announced by Deputy Prime Minister John Prescott, taxpayers were merely offered an account of the expenditures (£180 billion). Absent was a measure of the leakages and losses. A revised form of accounting is suggested in Table 5.

The estimate of leakages – the 'externalised' values that are siphoned through the land market – appears in column 4. This registers an unrealistically low minimum figure of £185 billion, which we base on the writings of a Nobel prize-winning economist, William Vickrey, who devoted his academic life to teaching at Columbia University, New York.

Vickrey was a lifelong student of the economics of transport systems in London and New York. He emphasised that land-owners could share the costs of public services by paying for the capital infrastructure, because the externalised values they captured were at least as great as the capital sum that needed to be invested to upgrade mass transit systems. In fact, it was in their financial interests to do so:

> Equity and efficiency are both served by having landlords contribute to the network costs of the services so as to enable their prices to be brought closer to marginal cost. In the long run the increased efficiency of the local economy would tend to redound to the benefit of the landlords by raising their market rents by more than the amount of the subsidy. (Vickrey, 1999: 23)[9]

But by how much more would rents rise as a result of the application of the optimising policy? Vickrey (ibid.: 25) did not suggest numbers for the upper limits of the gains in rent:

---

9   Vickrey actively canvassed the need to rebase public charges on economic rent, to deter (and therefore eliminate the losses from) the sub-optimal use of land.

Table 5 **The 10-Year Transport Plan**

*Investment and expenditure, 2002–011 (£bn outturn prices)**			*The impact of fiscal policy*	
Taxpayer-funded expenditures	Private investment	Total	Land value leakage	Dead-weight loss†
(1)	*(2)*	*(3)*	*(4)*	*(5)*

	Taxpayer-funded expenditures	Private investment	Total	Land value leakage	Dead-weight loss†
Road, railways & other transport	£124bn	£56bn	£180bn	Between £185bn and £540bn	Between £37bn and £248bn

* Derived from Department of Transport, 2000: 3

† Estimates draw on modelling by Tideman and Plassmann (1998) and Tideman et al. (2002)

> If landlords in a community could be made aware of their long-run interests, they would voluntarily agree to tax themselves on a site-value basis to subsidise utility rates so as to permit them to be set at close to the efficient level, and find that the rental value of their land had risen by *more than the amount of the tax subsidy*. (Emphasis added)

So even on this cautious assessment the amount that government spent on infrastructure would be covered by increases in rents. But the leakages of land value may be as high as £540 billion, if we take as our guide the uplift in values arising from new transport systems such as London's Jubilee Line Extension, which delivered a benefit-to-cost ratio of 3:1.

In addition to the leakages, we also have to factor in the deadweight losses from taxation. The range of the loss is shown in column 5 in Table 5. At a minimum, the UK would be deprived of wealth and welfare worth about £37 billion, if we use the Treasury's measure of the SOCEF. The loss rises to something like £248 billion if we use the comprehensive measure of deadweight losses proposed by economists such as Professors Tideman and Plassmann.

Thus, under the tax-based transport plan, the ten-year redistribution of income to prosperous property owners is on a horrendous scale. Not only are the poorest taxpayers likely to be non-owners of property and cars, but they also contribute disproportionately to the enhancement of the value of land owned by rich car owners.

The data in column 4 shows that sufficient *additional* value will be generated to at least cover the investment cost. *The capital investment in transport infrastructure pays for itself.* Under the optimal funding policy, *the transport projects would not need income to be redistributed from taxpayers.*

Retiring the bad taxes

It is exciting to contemplate the size of the transport windfalls in terms of the opportunity to abolish taxes that damage the nation's wealth and welfare.

If we adopt the benefit ratios identified in the seminal study by the European Conference of Ministers of Transport (ECMT), the ten-year spending plans could raise land values by a ratio of more than 3:1.[10] So if the plan were fully executed, the windfall for landowners could exceed £540 billion if the benefits were fully translated into increases in land values. By tapping just a part of

---

10   Members include the UK and 42 other European countries. There are seven associate members (Australia, Canada, Japan, Korea, Mexico, New Zealand and the USA).

such gains, the scope for reducing the taxes on labour and capital would be considerable. Adopting this financial strategy would transform transport into one of the leading sectors for structural reform. Individuals and firms, fully informed of the costs of their use of transportation, would make rational decisions about the levels of their demand for mobility (ECMT, 2003: 3). This begins to deliver the self-funding, integrated ideal. For the highways, for example, 'When congestion is present and charged for, the capital costs of roads will normally be recovered' (p. 9). The dividends, when measured on an economy-wide scale, are enormous. This is implied by the ECMT study *Reforming Transport Taxes*. The efficient way to raise revenue was defined in these terms: 'Charges on external costs. This requires users to pay for the benefits which they receive, as when they deposit waste in the environment. Efficiency and welfare neutral charges on economic rents and on the production of natural resources' (ibid.: 20). These contrasted with 'efficiency and welfare reducing taxes – most other forms of taxation'.

Europe's transport ministers wanted to know the scale of gains that would be achieved if governments set prices close to the point where users and other beneficiaries covered the costs. A model was needed to calculate the deadweight losses. Under current policies, the bias is towards the over-pricing and under-use of rail, and the under-pricing and over-use of urban roads. To reverse this situation it is necessary to deploy charges that do not exact an 'excess burden'. The ECMT proposed that distortionary taxes should be replaced by the efficient forms of charges, and deploying the gains 'to reduce the level of the distorting taxes' (ibid.: 22). It was argued:

Table 6 **Revenue and welfare changes from optimal pricing (€ billions per annum)**

Revenues	Britain	France	Germany	Total
Reference scenario revenues*	59.84	49.10	56.97	165.91
Optimal revenues	98.79	77.01	99.13	274.93
Absolute change in revenues	38.95	27.91	42.16	109.02
Percentage change	65	57	74	66
Welfare				
Absolute change in welfare	17.42	10.16	8.76	36.34

*The reference scenario is based on existing costs including estimated external costs, taxes, prices and traffic. These corresponded closely with official and published estimates of tax receipts for all the transport modes covered in each country.
Source: ECMT, 2003: table 1, p. 34

> For the benefits of optimising transport pricing by means of taxes on externalities do not accrue only within the transport sector in the form of a reduction in the levels of congestion, pollution and accidents. They also accrue to the larger society. The new revenues from externality taxes can be put to use *to reduce the level of welfare-reducing taxation for any given level of public expenditure*. (p. 31, emphasis added)

The ECMT researchers studied five countries, including the Netherlands and Finland, using data for 2000. The results for Britain, France and Germany are shown in Table 6.

The largest gains in both revenues and welfare were achieved in Britain. For the three countries, there was additional revenue of €109 billion per annum, and a €36 billion per annum net welfare gain. The welfare improvement is a *net* gain: what remains after deducting the reductions in some benefits enjoyed by motorists who are currently under-charged, and taking into account reductions in travel time for motorists and freight traffic in the newly decongested roads, reductions in pollution and accidents, and so on.

Table 7 **Cost recovery from optimal pricing (€ billions per annum)**

	Britain	France	Germany
Infrastructure costs with capital costs discounted at 6 per cent (C)*	22.50	36.04	27.10
Optimal revenues from all inland transport modes less VAT (R)	82.75	58.06	82.89
Cost recovery (R/C, %)	368	161	306

* Excluding air transport
Source: ECMT, 2003: table 6, p. 43

A second major finding concerns the capacity of transport systems to finance the costs of infrastructure. For three European countries the results are shown in Table 7: optimal revenues are sufficient to defray the fixed costs. In the case of Britain the cost recovery is 368 per cent, or a ratio of 3.7:1. Germany is not far behind with a ratio of 3:1.

The findings for Britain may be interpreted with reference to land values, which ultimately reflect most of the externalised costs and benefits. London's Jubilee Line Extension increased adjoining land values, according to Don Riley (2001: 23–5), by something close to £14 billion.[11] The JLE cost £3.4 billion to build.

At the very least, we can conclude that the application of optimal pricing and public finance policies would yield enormous material, social and environmental gains.

Optimal pricing enables governments to restructure national budgets. Such a strategy would be consistent with emerging thinking in Europe. The tax shift commended by the ECMT study endorses the marginal social costs pricing policy proposed by the European Commission (1998).

---

11   Subsequent studies commissioned by Transport for London found that the uplift in land values around just two of the JLE stations was of the order of £2.8 billion.

From these findings, we can draw two vital conclusions:

- The claim that a shortage of funds constrains investment in transport is spurious. The perception that there *is* a shortage springs from a philosophy of taxation that is at variance with economic reality.
- Subsidies from taxpayers are not needed. If people paid for the services they received at the locations they occupied, capital-intensive projects could be self-funding.

To secure a democratic consensus behind fiscal reform, however, people need to accept that the boundaries between rights and responsibilities must be renegotiated. This is not a novel proposal. Amendments to laws have occurred in the past in response to the changing needs of an evolving economy, as Adam Smith (1766 [1982]: 470) noted.[12]

Reforms would need to include safeguards for those who are at risk during the transitional period, but the personal incentives to change are overwhelming. The logic of the reform would be self-evident to people who demand value for their money. When people spend their earnings, £1 buys them £1's worth of goods or satisfaction. When government spends people's money, the real value of its £1 drops to 70p (if you accept the Treasury yardstick), or that value is completely negated, if we accept the estimates of independent economists.

---

12 Adam Smith draws attention to what happened when, with the development of markets, it was necessary to construct highways through private estates. Originally, rights of way were of a personal character, but these could not serve a complex commercial society. It was necessary for the law to be amended so that servitudes were transformed into real rights which could be enforced against the proprietors of land.

This loss is plugged if Adam Smith's optimum policy for public revenue is adopted.

One test of efficient governance, then, is the financial one: £1 spent by government must be as valuable as £1 spent by the person who earned it. This is the imperative to which government needs to aspire. When it is achieved, society would be presented with a new range of remarkable options. One would be the choice of reducing state provision of services. Responsibility for personal health and education was transferred to the welfare state because the leakages and losses made it impossible for millions of people to pay for these themselves. But the 60-year experiment in welfare statism has failed to deliver on its promise to close the gap between the rich and the poor.

To remain competitive, Britain must embark on meaningful fiscal reform. Ultimately, what matters is not *how much* is raised by taxation so much as *how* it is raised. A new paradigm is needed for the post-industrial society. We can now visualise the contours of that alternative. At its cutting edge would be the freedom of people to invest in their country's infrastructure. Hong Kong, which was a British initiative, provides one model for this prospectus.

The wheels of fortune are currently moving in China's direction, in the process further eroding Europe's manufacturing base. There is evidence that dynamic regions in China, such as Shenchen, are already using the optimum pricing/funding model for city infrastructure to support their booming property development. Privately funded highways are being added to the nation's transport infrastructure, and private capital from the West is now being sought to upgrade the state railways (Dickie, 2005; Dickie and Guerrera, 2005; Gapper, 2005). If China were to adopt such policies throughout her territory, economic survival for countries like Britain would depend on the willingness to match that one reform.

China is developing a model that combines lower labour and land costs with a lower tax burden. That combination is lethal. In response, the West should resist the easy temptations of protectionism. The solution is to retire its obsolete tax-driven strategies. Otherwise, our cities could be reduced to hollowed-out satellites of the dynamic Asian economies, struggling outposts of the Chinese manufacturing machine. For example, we can visualise the prospect of Asian-owned mega retail parks being built on exhausted gravel pits in Kent, selling imported clothes and consumer durables direct to consumers and cutting out British middlemen. Those consumers could be shuttled in every fifteen minutes on the privately owned Paradise Express from Canary Wharf II, a terminus that channels people away from the West End and London suburban shopping centres.

The expertise to exploit the synergy that flows from an integrated transport/retail nexus already exists in the Far East (see Chapter 4 above). It is even now being offered to Britain and Germany by Hong Kong's MTR Corporation (Wright 2005). By harnessing such experience, a new golden age could dawn for Britain, but this will not be achieved through government exhortation. Rather, we should trust the natural talents of our entrepreneurs and their employees. Once liberated from the burden of taxation, they would have all the incentives in the world to secure Britain's share of the looming global prosperity.

REFERENCES

Anderson, R. (2004), 'PPPs "no panacea" for the EU's new members', *Financial Times*, 1 March.

Armstrong, M., S. Cowan and J. Vickers (1994), *Regulatory Reform: Economic Analysis and British Experience*, Cambridge, MA: MIT Press.

Association of Train Operating Companies (2005), *Looking Forward: Contribution to the Railway Strategy*, London: ATOC.

Bannister, B. (1994), *Transport Planning in the UK, USA and Europe*, London: E. & F. N. Spon.

Bates, J., J. Polak, P. Jones and A. Cook (2001), 'The valuation of reliability for personal travel', *Transportation Research Part E: Logistics and Transportation Review*, 37: 191–229.

Belloc, H. (1923), *The Road*, Manchester: Charles W. Hobson.

Blitz, R. (2004), 'Crossrail to give economy £19 billion boost, say studies', *Financial Times*, 3 February.

Bowker, R. (2005), 'To buy or not to buy', *RAIL*, 11–24 May.

Boxell, J. (2005), 'BA chief slams "protectionist" US', *Financial Times*, 23 September.

Bream, R. (2004), 'Call for commuters to pay higher train fares to ease burden on taxpayers', *Financial Times*, 12 February.

British Chambers of Commerce (2004), *Getting Business Moving: A Transport Survey*, London: British Chambers of Commerce.

Brittan, S. (2003), 'Brown will stick to his own rules', *Financial Times*, 21 November.

Calderbank, G. (2001), *Canal, Coal, & Tramway: An Introduction to the Industrial Heritage of Mamble*, Moreton-on-Lugg: L. C. Promotion.

Channon, P. (1989), 'Preface' in *Central London Rail Study*, London: Department of Transport/BR Network South East, London Regional Transport and London Underground Ltd.

Clark, A. (2004), 'EuroTunnel begs for rescue plan', *Guardian*, 12 February.

Clark, A. (2005), 'Network Rail leaves £1 billion repairs undone', *Guardian*, 8 June.

Clementi, A. (2003), *Infrascape*, Florence: Mandragora.

Commission for Integrated Transport (2001), *European Best Practice in Delivering Integrated Transport*, London: Commission for Integrated Transport.

Commission for Integrated Transport (2004), *High-Speed Rail*, London: Commission for Integrated Transport.

Crow, B. (2003), 'The vandals are in retreat', *Guardian*, 5 November.

Deininger, K. (2003), *Land Policies for Growth and Poverty Reduction*, Washington, DC: World Bank and Oxford University Press.

Department for Transport (2004), 'Guidance on value for money', London: Department for Transport.

Department of the Environment, Transport and the Regions (2000), *Transport 2010: The 10-Year Plan*, London: DETR.

Department of Transport et al. (1990), *Central London Rail Study – a Report on Further Work*, London: TSO.

Department of Transport (2000), '£180 billion ten year investment plan to deliver top class transport system', news release, 20 July.

Dickie, M. (2005), 'Foreign investors poised to be asked to come aboard', *Financial Times*, 1 November.

Dickie, M. and F. Guerrera (2005), 'China's railways lined up for listing', *Financial Times*, 1 November.

ECMT (European Conference of Ministers of Transport) (2003), *Reforming Transport Taxes*, Paris: OECD.

European Commission (1998), *Fair Payment for Infrastructure Use: A Phased Approach to a Common Transport Infrastructure Charging Framework for the EU*, White Paper, Brussels: European Commission.

Ferguson, N. (ed.) (1997), *Virtual History: Alternatives and Counterfactuals*, London: Picador.

Flürscheim, M. (n.d.), *Clue to the Economic Labyrinth*, London: Swan Sonnenschein

Foldvary, F. (2005) 'Infrastructure: optimal private and governmental funding and provision', *Economic Affairs*, 25(1): 25–30.

Gaffney, M. (1964), 'Containment policies for urban sprawl', in R. Stauber (ed.), *Approaches to the Study of Urbanization*, Governmental Research Center, University of Kansas.

Gaffney, M. (1969), 'Land planning and the property tax', *Journal of the American Institute of Planners*, 35(3): 178–83.

Gaffney, M. (1970), 'Urban expansion – will it ever stop?', in R. G. Putnam, F. J. Taylor and P. G. Kettle (eds), *A Geography of Urban Places*, Toronto: Methuen.

Gaffney, M. (1972), 'Land rent, taxation and public policy #i: sources, nature and function of urban land rent', *American Journal of Economics and Sociology*, 31(3): 241–58.

Gaffney, M. (1973), 'Land rent, taxation and public policy #ii: taxation and the functions of urban land rent', *American Journal of Economics and Sociology*, 32(1): 17–34.

Gaffney M. (1988), 'Non-point pollution: tractable solutions to intractable problems', *Journal of Business Administration*, 18: 133–54.

Gaffney, M. (1998), 'An inventory of rent-yielding resources', in F. Harrison (ed.), *The Losses of Nations*, London: Othila Press.

Gaffney, M. (2001), 'How to revive a dying city', in C. Cobb and J. Giacalone (eds), *The Path to Justice*, Oxford: Blackwell.

Gapper, J. (2005), 'The contradiction in China's capitalist line', *Financial Times*, 3 November.

Giles, C. (2005), 'Debt move narrows Brown's options', *Financial Times*, 20 May.

Halcrow Fox & Associates (1989), *East London Rail Study Report*, London: Department of Transport.

Halliday, S. (2001), *Underground to Everywhere*, London: Sutton Publishing.

Harrison, A. J. (1974), *The Economics of Transport Appraisal*, London: Croom Helm.

Harrison, F. (1983), *The Power in the Land*, London: Shepheard-Walwyn.

Harrison, F. (2003), 'Manna from heaven: radio rent windfalls and the Tax Conversion Fund', *Geophilos*, 3 (1), available from www.landresearchtrust.org.

Harrison, F. (2005), *Boom Bust: House Prices, Banking and the Depression of 2010*, London: Shepheard-Walwyn.

Hawke, G. R. (1970), *Railways and Economic Growth in England and Wales 1840–1870*, Oxford: Clarendon Press.

Heatley, B. (2000), 'How a canal almost came to Ludlow', *Journal of the Railway and Canal Historical Society*, 39(6).

Heritage Foundation (2003), *Index of Economic Freedom*, Washington, DC: Heritage Foundation/Dow Jones.

Hibbs, J. (1982), *Transport without Politics … ?*, Hobart Paper 95, London: Institute of Economic Affairs.

HM Treasury (2003), *UK Membership of the Single Currency*, London: TSO.

HM Treasury (2005), *Budget 2005: Financial Statement & Budget Report*, London: HM Treasury.

Holbrook, S. (1947), *The Story of American Railroads*, New York: Crown Publishers.

House of Commons Transport Select Committee (2003), *Jam Tomorrow?: The Multi Modal Study Investment Plans*, London: TSO.

House of Commons Transport Select Committee (2004), *The Future of the Railway*, 7th report of session 2003/04, vol. 1, London: TSO.

Jansen, M. (2003), 'A fair share', *Property Week*, 24 October.

Jones Lang Wootton (1989), *Funding of the Jubilee Line Extension: The Canary Wharf Case*, London, Jones Lang Wootton.

Kirkaldy, A. W. and A. D. Evans (1931), *The History and Economics of Transport*, London: Pitman.

Kopicki, R., L. S. Thompson et al. (1995), *Best Methods of Railway Restructuring and Privatisation*, Washington, DC: World Bank.

Labour Research Department (1950), *Facts and Figures for Socialists 1951*, London: Labour Party Research Department.

Lau, J. (2005), 'Property gains help to lift MTR', *Financial Times*, 3 August.

Lefmann, O. and K. K. Larsen (2000), 'Denmark', in R. V. Andelson, *Land-value Taxation around the World*, 3rd edn, Oxford: Blackwell.

Livingstone, K. (2004), 'Why Crossrail should proceed without delay', *Financial Times*, 2 February.

Meek, J. (2004), 'The £10 billion rail crash', *Guardian* G2, 1 April.

Ministry of Land, Infrastructure and Transport (2002), *Summary of White Paper on Land*, Tokyo: MLIT.

Moorsom, N. (1975), *The Stockton & Darlington Railway: The Foundation of Middlesbrough*, Middlesbrough: J. G. Peckston.

Moules, J. (2005), 'Cost of business regulation could exceed tax revenue', *Financial Times*, 4 July.

MTR Corporation (n.d.), *MTR Corporation: An introduction*, Hong Kong: MTR Corporation.

Müller, A. and G. Mørch-Lassen (1989), 'Land valuation and fiscal policy in Denmark', in R. Banks (ed.), *Costing the Earth*, London: Shepheard-Walwyn.

Myers, N. (1999), 'Perverse subsidies', *RSA Journal*, 3/4.

Noland, R. B. and J. W. Polak (2002), 'Travel time variability: a review of theoretical and empirical issues', *Transport Reviews*, 22.

O'Neil, M. A., A. J. Palmer and R. Beggs (1998), 'The effects of survey timing on perceptions of service quality', *Managing Service Quality*, 8.

Osborne, A. (2005), 'Byers looked into pulling plug on Railtrack earlier', *Daily Telegraph*, 13 June.

Plender, J. (2004), 'One tax to untangle this unholy mess', *Estates Gazette*, 28 February.

Reed, P. (2002), *Railtracks in the Sky*, Nottingham: Spokesman.

Ricardo, D. (1817), *On the Principles of Political Economy and Taxation*, London: John Murray.

Ricketts, M. (2005), 'Property rights, incentives and privatization', in S. Roy and J. Clarke (eds), *Margaret Thatcher's Revolution*, London: Continuum.

Riley, D. (2001), *Taken for a Ride*, London: Centre for Land Policy Studies.

Riley, D. (2003), 'Financing transport projects through land value gains: how do developers view this? Perspective 2', Waterfront Conference, London, 20 May.

Roberts, H. (2005), *Life in Britain: Using millennial census data to understand poverty, inequality and place*, York: Joseph Rowntree Foundation.

Roy, R. (1998), *Infrastructure Cost Recovery under Allocatively Efficient Pricing*, UIC/CER Economic Expert Study: Final Report, London/Paris: UIC.

Roy, R. (2003), *Postponing the Future*, London: Railway Forum.

Roy, R. (2005), 'Optimal pricing: the route to a self-funding infrastructure – and more', *Economic Affairs*, 25(1): 5–11.

Samuelson, P. A. and W. D. Nordhaus (1985), *Economics*, 12th edn., New York: McGraw-Hill.

Schabas, M. (1994), 'Burnt offering', *New Civil Engineer*, 10 March.

Sheppard, Lord et al. (2003), 'Transport infrastructure needs long-term funds', Letters, *Financial Times*, 8 December.

Smith, A. (1776 [1981]), *An Inquiry into the Nature and Causes of the Wealth of Nations*, ed. R. H. Campbell and A. Skinner, Indianapolis: Liberty Fund.

Smith, A. (1766 [1982]), *Lectures on Jurisprudence*, ed. R. L. Meek,
D. D. Raphael and P. G. Stein, Indianapolis: Liberty Fund.

Sweezy, P. M. (1938), *Monopoly and Competition in the English Coal
Trade, 1550–1850*, London: Greenwood Press.

Thomas, D. (2003), *Strategic Options for Financing and Procuring
Major Transport Projects*, London, 19 November.

Tideman, N. and F. Plassmann (1998), 'Taxed out of work and
wealth: the costs of taxing labour and capital', in F. Harrison
(ed.), *The Losses of Nations*, London: Othila Press.

Tideman, N. et al. (2002), 'The avoidable excess burden of broad-
based US taxes', *Public Finance Review*, 30(5): 416–41.

Town & Country Planning Association (1999), *People, Where Will
They Work?*, London: Town & Country Planning Association.

Vickrey, W. (1999), four chapters in K. C. Wenzer (ed.),
Land-value Taxation, Armonk, NY/London: M. E. Sharp/
Shepheard-Walwyn.

Walsh, C. (2004), 'Why slot sales are key to airlines' take-off',
Observer Business, 11 April.

Warn, K. (2003), 'Canada's fittest location', *Financial Times*, 9
August.

Wassenbergh, H. A. (1957), *Post-war International Civil Aviation
Policy and the Law of the Air*, The Hague: Martinus Nijhoff.

Welsh, F. (1997), *A History of Hong Kong*, London: HarperCollins.

Wilkinson, P. (2001), *What the Romans Did for Us*, London:
Macmillan.

Williams, F. (2004), 'Poor countries worst hit by road accident
deaths', *Financial Times*, 7 April.

Williams, F. (2005), 'Warning on trade "quality barriers"',
Financial Times, 22 June.

Willoughby, C. (2000), *Singapore's Experience in Managing Motorization, and Its Relevance to Other Countries*, Washington, DC: World Bank, available at www.worldbank.org/transport/publicat/twu43_ab.htm.

Winfrey, R. (1969), *Economic Analysis for Highways*, Scranton, PA: International Textbook Co.

Womack, S. (2005), 'Rich–poor divide "as wide as 60 years ago"', *Daily Telegraph*, 2 September.

World Bank (2000), *Private Solutions for Infrastructure: Opportunities for the Philippines*, Washington, DC: World Bank.

Wright, R. (2005), 'MTR looks to run Germany's S-Bahns', *Financial Times*, 14 November.

Yarmey, A. D. (2000), 'Retrospective duration estimations for variant and invariant events in field situations', *Applied Cognitive Psychology*, 14(1): 45–57.

Yen, J. R., C. H. Teng and P. S. Chen (2001), 'Measuring the level of services at airport passenger terminals – comparison of perceived and observed time', *Transportation Research Record*, National Research Council, USA.

ABOUT THE IEA

The Institute is a research and educational charity (No. CC 235 351), limited by guarantee. Its mission is to improve understanding of the fundamental institutions of a free society with particular reference to the role of markets in solving economic and social problems.

The IEA achieves its mission by:

- a high-quality publishing programme
- conferences, seminars, lectures and other events
- outreach to school and college students
- brokering media introductions and appearances

The IEA, which was established in 1955 by the late Sir Antony Fisher, is an educational charity, not a political organisation. It is independent of any political party or group and does not carry on activities intended to affect support for any political party or candidate in any election or referendum, or at any other time. It is financed by sales of publications, conference fees and voluntary donations.

In addition to its main series of publications the IEA also publishes a quarterly journal, *Economic Affairs*.

The IEA is aided in its work by a distinguished international Academic Advisory Council and an eminent panel of Honorary Fellows. Together with other academics, they review prospective IEA publications, their comments being passed on anonymously to authors. All IEA papers are therefore subject to the same rigorous independent refereeing process as used by leading academic journals.

IEA publications enjoy widespread classroom use and course adoptions in schools and universities. They are also sold throughout the world and often translated/reprinted.

Since 1974 the IEA has helped to create a world-wide network of 100 similar institutions in over 70 countries. They are all independent but share the IEA's mission.

Views expressed in the IEA's publications are those of the authors, not those of the Institute (which has no corporate view), its Managing Trustees, Academic Advisory Council members or senior staff.

Members of the Institute's Academic Advisory Council, Honorary Fellows, Trustees and Staff are listed on the following page.

The Institute gratefully acknowledges financial support for its publications programme and other work from a generous benefaction by the late Alec and Beryl Warren.

187

Other papers recently published by the IEA include:

WHO, What and Why?

Transnational Government, Legitimacy and the World Health Organization
Roger Scruton
Occasional Paper 113; ISBN 0 255 36487 3
£8.00

The World Turned Rightside Up

A New Trading Agenda for the Age of Globalisation
John C. Hulsman
Occasional Paper 114; ISBN 0 255 36495 4
£8.00

The Representation of Business in English Literature

Introduced and edited by Arthur Pollard
Readings 53; ISBN 0 255 36491 1
£12.00

Anti-Liberalism 2000

The Rise of New Millennium Collectivism
David Henderson
Occasional Paper 115; ISBN 0 255 36497 0
£7.50

Capitalism, Morality and Markets

Brian Griffiths, Robert A. Sirico, Norman Barry & Frank Field
Readings 54; ISBN 0 255 36496 2
£7.50

A Conversation with Harris and Seldon
Ralph Harris & Arthur Seldon
Occasional Paper 116; ISBN 0 255 36498 9
£7.50

Malaria and the DDT Story
Richard Tren & Roger Bate
Occasional Paper 117; ISBN 0 255 36499 7
£10.00

A Plea to Economists Who Favour Liberty: Assist the Everyman
Daniel B. Klein
Occasional Paper 118; ISBN 0 255 36501 2
£10.00

The Changing Fortunes of Economic Liberalism
Yesterday, Today and Tomorrow
David Henderson
Occasional Paper 105 (new edition); ISBN 0 255 36520 9
£12.50

The Global Education Industry
Lessons from Private Education in Developing Countries
James Tooley
Hobart Paper 141 (new edition); ISBN 0 255 36503 9
£12.50

Saving Our Streams

The Role of the Anglers' Conservation Association in
Protecting English and Welsh Rivers
Roger Bate
Research Monograph 53; ISBN 0 255 36494 6
£10.00

Better Off Out?

The Benefits or Costs of EU Membership
Brian Hindley & Martin Howe
Occasional Paper 99 (new edition); ISBN 0 255 36502 0
£10.00

Buckingham at 25

Freeing the Universities from State Control
Edited by James Tooley
Readings 55; ISBN 0 255 36512 8
£15.00

Lectures on Regulatory and Competition Policy

Irwin M. Stelzer
Occasional Paper 120; ISBN 0 255 36511 X
‚12.50

Misguided Virtue

False Notions of Corporate Social Responsibility
David Henderson
Hobart Paper 142; ISBN 0 255 36510 1
£12.50

HIV and Aids in Schools

The Political Economy of Pressure Groups and Miseducation
Barrie Craven, Pauline Dixon, Gordon Stewart & James Tooley
Occasional Paper 121; ISBN 0 255 36522 5
£10.00

The Road to Serfdom

The Reader's Digest *condensed version*
Friedrich A. Hayek
Occasional Paper 122; ISBN 0 255 36530 6
£7.50

Bastiat's *The Law*

Introduction by Norman Barry
Occasional Paper 123; ISBN 0 255 36509 8
£7.50

A Globalist Manifesto for Public Policy

Charles Calomiris
Occasional Paper 124; ISBN 0 255 36525 X
£7.50

Euthanasia for Death Duties

Putting Inheritance Tax Out of Its Misery
Barry Bracewell-Milnes
Research Monograph 54; ISBN 0 255 36513 6
£10.00

Liberating the Land

The Case for Private Land-use Planning
Mark Pennington
Hobart Paper 143; ISBN 0 255 36508 x
£10.00

IEA Yearbook of Government Performance 2002/2003

Edited by Peter Warburton
Yearbook 1; ISBN 0 255 36532 2
£15.00

Britain's Relative Economic Performance, 1870– 1999

Nicholas Crafts
Research Monograph 55; ISBN 0 255 36524 1
£10.00

Should We Have Faith in Central Banks?

Otmar Issing
Occasional Paper 125; ISBN 0 255 36528 4
£7.50

The Dilemma of Democracy

Arthur Seldon
Hobart Paper 136 (reissue); ISBN 0 255 36536 5
£10.00

Capital Controls: a 'Cure' Worse Than the Problem?

Forrest Capie

Research Monograph 56; ISBN 0 255 36506 3

£10.00

The Poverty of 'Development Economics'

Deepak Lal

Hobart Paper 144 (reissue); ISBN 0 255 36519 5

£15.00

Should Britain Join the Euro?

The Chancellor's Five Tests Examined

Patrick Minford

Occasional Paper 126; ISBN 0 255 36527 6

£7.50

Post-Communist Transition: Some Lessons

Leszek Balcerowicz

Occasional Paper 127; ISBN 0 255 36533 0

£7.50

A Tribute to Peter Bauer

John Blundell et al.

Occasional Paper 128; ISBN 0 255 36531 4

£10.00

Employment Tribunals

Their Growth and the Case for Radical Reform

J. R. Shackleton

Hobart Paper 145; ISBN 0 255 36515 2

£10.00

Fifty Economic Fallacies Exposed

Geoffrey E. Wood
Occasional Paper 129; ISBN 0 255 36518 7
£12.50

A Market in Airport Slots

Keith Boyfield (editor), David Starkie, Tom Bass & Barry Humphreys
Readings 56; ISBN 0 255 36505 5
£10.00

Money, Inflation and the Constitutional Position of the Central Bank

Milton Friedman & Charles A. E. Goodhart
Readings 57; ISBN 0 255 36538 1
£10.00

railway.com

Parallels between the Early British Railways and the ICT Revolution
Robert C. B. Miller
Research Monograph 57; ISBN 0 255 36534 9
£12.50

The Regulation of Financial Markets

Edited by Philip Booth & David Currie
Readings 58; ISBN 0 255 36551 9
£12.50

Climate Alarmism Reconsidered
Robert L. Bradley Jr
Hobart Paper 146; ISBN 0 255 36541 1
£12.50

Government Failure: E. G. West on Education
Edited by James Tooley & James Stanfield
Occasional Paper 130; ISBN 0 255 36552 7
£12.50

Waging the War of Ideas
John Blundell
Second edition
Occasional Paper 131; ISBN 0 255 36547 0
£12.50

**Corporate Governance: Accountability in
the Marketplace**
Elaine Sternberg
Second edition
Hobart Paper 147; ISBN 0 255 36542 X
£12.50

The Land Use Planning System
Evaluating Options for Reform
John Corkindale
Hobart Paper 148; ISBN 0 255 36550 0
£10.00

Economy and Virtue

Essays on the Theme of Markets and Morality
Edited by Dennis O'Keeffe
Readings 59; ISBN 0 255 36504 7
£12.50

Free Markets Under Siege

Cartels, Politics and Social Welfare
Richard A. Epstein
Occasional Paper 132; ISBN 0 255 36553 5
£10.00

Unshackling Accountants

D. R. Myddelton
Hobart Paper 149; ISBN 0 255 36559 4
£12.50

The Euro as Politics

Pedro Schwartz
Research Monograph 58; ISBN 0 255 36535 7
£12.50

Pricing Our Roads

Vision and Reality
Stephen Glaister & Daniel J. Graham
Research Monograph 59; ISBN 0 255 36562 4
£10.00

The Role of Business in the Modern World

Progress, Pressures, and Prospects for the Market Economy
David Henderson
Hobart Paper 150; ISBN 0 255 36548 9
£12.50

Public Service Broadcasting Without the BBC?

Alan Peacock
Occasional Paper 133; ISBN 0 255 36565 9
£10.00

The ECB and the Euro: the First Five Years

Otmar Issing
Occasional Paper 134; ISBN 0 255 36555 1
£10.00

Towards a Liberal Utopia?

Edited by Philip Booth
Hobart Paperback 32; ISBN 0 255 36563 2
£15.00

The Way Out of the Pensions Quagmire

Philip Booth & Deborah Cooper
Research Monograph 60; ISBN 0 255 36517 9
£12.50

Black Wednesday

A Re-examination of Britain's Experience in the Exchange Rate Mechanism
Alan Budd
Occasional Paper 135; ISBN 0 255 36566 7
£7.50

Crime: Economic Incentives and Social Networks
Paul Ormerod
Hobart Paper 151; ISBN 0 255 36554 3
£10.00

The Road to Serfdom *with* The Intellectuals and Socialism
Friedrich A. Hayek
Occasional Paper 136; ISBN 0 255 36576 4
£10.00

Money and Asset Prices in Boom and Bust
Tim Congdon
Hobart Paper 152; ISBN 0 255 36570 5
£10.00

The Dangers of Bus Re-regulation
and Other Perspectives on Markets in Transport
John Hibbs et al.
Occasional Paper 137; ISBN 0 255 36572 1
£10.00

The New Rural Economy
Change, Dynamism and Government Policy
Berkeley Hill et al.
Occasional Paper 138; ISBN 0 255 36546 2
£15.00

The Benefits of Tax Competition
Richard Teather
Hobart Paper 153; ISBN 0 255 36569 1
£12.50

To order copies of currently available IEA papers, or to enquire about availability, please contact:

Gazelle
IEA orders
FREEPOST RLYS-EAHU-YSCZ
White Cross Mills
Hightown
Lancaster LA1 4XS

Tel: 01524 68765
Fax: 01524 63232
Email: sales@gazellebooks.co.uk

The IEA also offers a subscription service to its publications. For a single annual payment, currently £40.00 in the UK, you will receive every monograph the IEA publishes during the course of a year and discounts on our extensive back catalogue. For more information, please contact:

Adam Myers
Subscriptions
The Institute of Economic Affairs
2 Lord North Street
London SW1P 3LB

Tel: 020 7799 8920
Fax: 020 7799 2137
Website: www.iea.org.uk